CHASING DAKAR

A Rider's Guide to Adventure Riding, Rally Preparation and Racing

By Johnathan Edwards, MD
and Scot Harden

PHOTO CREDITS:

Stephan Legrand
Lebig Productions LLC
www.lebigproductions.com

Jon Beck
www.jonbeckphotography.com

Scott Cox
Resource Marketing
www.resmarket.com

Mark Karyia
E-mail: kato4moto@aol.com

Jean Aignan Museau
Edition La Riviere
Moto Revue
12 Rue Mozart
Clichy, France 92587
E-mail: Jam@editions-lariviere.fr

KTM Corporation. All photos from www.ktmimages.com were the work of
the following photographers: Pierro Batini, Thorsten Flechsig, H. Mitterbauer,
H. Peuker, and G. Soldano

Maindruphotos
www.maindruphoto.com

Thomas McDonald, David Rauseo and Joe Barker

Front cover photos by H. Peuker (top) and Johnathan Edwards (bottom)
Front cover design by Scott Cox, Resource Marketing
Back cover photos by Johnathan Edwards and Scott Cox
Back cover design by Deborah Truscott
Title page photo by H. Peuker

CHASING DAKAR
A rider's guide to adventure riding and rally racing

By Johnathan Edwards, MD and Scot Harden

This book was designed by Deborah Truscott and printed by:
Goodway Graphics
6628 Electronic Drive
Springfield, VA 22151 USA

Copyright © 2006 by Johnathan Edwards
ISBN 0-9787094-0-3, print ed. 1.

PRINTED IN THE UNITED STATES OF AMERICA

Acknowledgements

Scot and I would like to thank the off-road riding community for many of the contributions to CHASING DAKAR. Without their help, this book would have not been possible.

Also a huge thanks the following people for help with their spectacular photographs: Stephan Legrand, Scott Cox, Joe Barker, Jonathan Beck, Jean Aignan Museau, David Rauseo, Mark Karyia, H. Peuker, Thorsten Flechsig, H. Mitterbauer, G. Soldano, J. Cunha, Thomas McDonald and Pierro Batini.

The following people read the manuscript and offered valuable input: Joe Barker, Charles Earl, James Embro and Stan Freeman. I especially want to thank Charles Earl, Joe Barker and Danielle Larson for their efforts in the preparation of this book.

Thanks to my very good friend, Guy Perotti, who helped me reach my goal in writing and publishing this book.

Johnathan Edwards, MD
June 2006

In memory of my mother

Susan Edwards

2/28/49 – 9/11/01

*She always encouraged me to write
and would have been so proud.*

Contents

Preface

Photo by Jean Aignan Museau.

Dakar, the final stop for the Dakar Rally, is a land rich in African culture, a privilege only for those who have completed the journey. Dakar represents a monumental feeling of accomplishment to the competitors, similar to climbing Mount Everest. Perhaps the ultimate in adventure riding, the Dakar Rally changes a person forever. Likewise, the joy of adventure riding changes a person; it is a reason each of us yearn to explore the ends of the earth on a motorcycle. Adventure riding truly is an expression of the human spirit, and the personality of the Dakar Rally is a living example. One time a year, the competitors totally put aside their artificial modern lives, and exist face to face with humanity staring directly into their souls; it is in the Dakar Rally where the will and the spirit are continually challenged. The joy, pain, and humility are revealed in each person, for it is the face of Africa.

The aim of this book is to give you a practical and holistic approach to rally and adventure off-road riding. We are providing you a road map from those who have gone before us, giving you the tools needed to complete this journey. In addition, by teaching basic and advanced skills of adventure and rally riding, you will have the fundamentals necessary to experience the world of off-road adventure riding in its purest and most passionate form.

*Johnathan Edwards and
Scot Harden*

Foreword

Photo by Scott Cox.

I'm often asked, What does it take to win? It's a simple answer. Preparation. Perseverance.

And a little luck.

After winning the Roof of Africa on a motorcycle and in a buggy as well at the Atlas Rally in Morocco, I was asked to participate in the Paris Dakar Rally in 1987. I jumped at the chance. But I was in for a surprise.

I found myself in the most remote, exciting, and adventurous landscape I had ever seen. My team and I were strangers in a foreign land, not expected to win—hardly expected to finish. But we persevered, trying to keep our wits about us as we pulled out all our tricks: pit crews, chase planes, mental endurance. The desert answered: relentless heat, sand storms, and its most frightening weapon—desolation.

"Don't get lost." It sounds like simple enough advice, but I assure you, you've not felt loneliness until you've driven for hours without seeing another soul, climbed to the top of the highest dune, put army-grade binoculars to your eyes and conducted a 360° pan.

Sand. Nothing but sand.

But that's the Paris Dakar Rally. That's what makes it special. The adventure. The excitement. The thrill of counting on not just yourself, but your team and the thousands of hours you've spent preparing for every possible curve the race may throw at you.

I finished fourth overall. It was unlike any event I had ever raced before or since. I consider it one of my proudest accomplishments.

The following pages are for everyone, from those planning to participate to those who have only dreamt of it. I wish this book had been published before I raced the Paris Dakar Rally. It would have saved me money, stress, and most importantly… *time*. Because in racing, time is all that matters. It's easy to go fast over twenty minutes; it's much harder to go fast over twenty days. The difference? Preparation. Perseverance.

And a little luck.

Malcolm Smith

Malcolm Smith Motorsports
Riverside, CA
www.malcolmsmith.com

Chapter 1

ADVENTURE, RALLY, AND LONG DISTANCE OFF-ROAD RIDING...

AN OFF-ROAD RIDER'S PERSPECTIVE

Follow your bliss ~ Joseph Campbell

Photo by H. Peuker.

Jacky Ickx, the legendary Formula 1 champion, explains with passion why the Dakar Rally is a race like none other: "The Dakar Rally is a true cure for those in search of youth. To finish, one must possess the fundamental desire to succeed, because the race brings out the person, and by the end, that person is changed forever." The system we live in forces us to exist in an artificial world. Once a year the rally offers to the competitor a perspective of life outside of the modern world and a chance to return to the basics. It forces one to deal with nature and the desert, while looking directly into the face of the human race.

The how and why we go adventure riding

Anyone who rides a motorcycle can attest to the reasons why we explore life on two wheels. For many, riding a motorcycle is "following your bliss," thus the reason many of us desire to explore new trails, to experience the freedom and to share our stories. That quote is one reason for writing this book. Motorcycle riding involves risk and sometimes can be viewed by the world as irrational decision making. Most adventure riders yearn for more in life, and they attempt to find it through riding a motorcycle. Riding a motorcycle gives a

The 2005 USA KTM Red Bull Dakar Team launches off a sand dune in Tunisia. (Photo by H. Peuker.)

person a sense of freedom not duplicated elsewhere.

Whatever the reason, we hope to provide a road map from those who have gone before us and the tools you will need to successfully reach this goal.

Is it the danger or adventure?

We are often asked the question, what is our motivation for riding and racing? After all, the sport is dangerous and people can actually lose their lives. To answer this, Rick Johnson, in the movie, "Dust to Glory," gives a very vivid response:

"Racers do not race because they have a death wish or something like that. It is not because we are crazy; rather, it is because of the competition. Being fighters, we do not fight to

Adventure riding at its core is about exploring new places. (Photo by Stephan Legrand.)

hurt people or ourselves—we fight only to win. Racers do not race because they want to be hurt; they want to go fast and be free. This is the euphoria of off-road racers. It is the way we manipulate life—through the mechanics of a machine. Off-road racing is a bit like chasing rainbows, endangering oneself for glory. People ask me, would

I quit racing if something bad happened? Why quit something, when you cannot stop life because something bad happens to you? People do not stop flying because of 9-11."

Adventure riding allows one to cover vast terrain, sharing the experience with fellow enthusiasts, changing the human spirit. After the adventure ride or rally, a person's outlook on life changes forever. Adventure riders yearn for different experiences. The chance to be in nature and reflect on oneself and the world are reasons for choosing adventure riding. Nature has been described as a pathway to a more divine sense of being; if you follow the footsteps nature has set out, it will lead to a better understanding of this divine sense. Following your senses on a motorcycle, respecting nature and all that you appreciate from adventure riding, is what makes it a unique experience.

Covering vast terrain and sharing the experience with others, adventure riding gives a freedom not duplicated anywhere else. (Photo by Stephan Legrand.)

Photo by H. Peuker.

Scot Harden and many others host adventure camps where riders from many different backgrounds come looking for something new. Adventure riding means that the rider and motorcycle are self sufficient, which is different from other disciplines of motorcycle riding. Most rides involve various terrains and conditions. For example, Harden Off-Road hosts the "Nevada Rally Experience," which starts in the desert and finishes in the mountains of Nevada. Variables such as tire choice, gear selection, rider skill and physical conditioning become very important when planning an adventure ride.

The Dakar Rally

Rally racing has been around for decades. The word rally literally means "to find the way." The Dakar Rally is among the most famous of these races and is considered the Mount Everest of off-road racing. The difference between adventure

Nevada provides some of the best adventure riding around and is home to the Nevada Rally Experience. (Photo by Stephan Legrand.)

riding and rally racing is simple: an adventure ride involves finding the way through various conditions and terrain; a rally is a very long adventure ride combined with a race. It is essentially a mass movement of motorcycles, cars and trucks from place to place in an organized fashion over vast terrains usually not accessible by standard road vehicles. In fact, many riders compete in the Dakar Rally not to win the race, but just to complete the journey.

U.S. KTM Red Bull Dakar team rider Kellon Walch on his way to a stage win in the 2005 Dakar rally. (Photo by Johnathan Edwards.)

During the 2006 Dakar Rally press conference in Las Vegas, Nevada, a panel of participants, including Robby Gordon, Scot Harden, and a host of others, was asked the question: "Why the Dakar Rally and what do you think about it now that you have completed it?" The general response from the panel was that the preparation necessary for the rally and completing the journey is life changing. The Rally brings out the character of each person, who he or she really is, and how one responds to danger and nature. The rally is long, filled with exciting lands both exotic and sometimes mundane, crossing many different cultures.

Frenchman Thierry Sabine created the Paris to Dakar Rally in 1979. Today, the Dakar Rally starts in many other cities, such as Barcelona, Clermont Ferrand and Lisbon, and finishes in Dakar, the capital of Senegal. The Rally is traditionally run with cars, trucks and motorcycles; however, it has been attempted on everything from Vespas to huge 6-wheel drive trucks, and has been completed by both men and women. Many stories are told about the adventures, the passion and the competitors. It is a unique race where the great professionals of racing combine with amateurs in a single event. This is why the rally is one of the greatest sporting events of this century. No American has ever won the Dakar Rally, though many have tried, including riders like Danny Laporte, Chuck Stearns, Malcolm Smith, Jimmy Lewis, and Scot Harden.

Thierry Sabine set the ambiance for the rally that we have come to know today. He

Mechanics work tirelessly through the night in the bivouac during the Dakar rally. (Photo by Pierro Batini.)

Adventure riding is very rewarding and can be experienced alone or shared amongst friends. (Photo by Scott Cox.)

fuel service and meals for the 2000 people who inhabit the bivouac daily.

Return to the human adventure

The Dakar Rally is truly a test of human endurance where motorcycles, cars and trucks pass through deserts, sand dunes, rocks, villages and many different cultures. It usually spans over 10,000 kilometers (6,200 miles) in about 20 days. The biggest challenges are the desert and endurance, according to Jean-Louis Schlesser, a long time competitor of the rally.

An incredible race unlike any other, one observes the environment, the preparation of each competitor, their habits,

was the leader, the Samaritan, the one everybody looked to for guidance. During the Paris to Dakar Rally in 1986, he tragically died for his passion in a helicopter crash. Expanding into one of the greatest races of this century, the Dakar Rally is a fully televised event, with air transportation, medical hospital,

The seemingly neverending sand dunes encountered in Africa make these found in North American small in comparison. (Photo by DPPI.)

An American Dakar rally hopeful, Chris Blais explodes off a sand dune in Tunisia. (Photo by H. Peuker.)

their ingenuity, the inventions and the immense character of the rally; each day, every person can count their experiences. It gives us a taste of adventure, breaking out of the everyday life and discovering other things.

Most notable about the Dakar Rally is that each competitor is changed forever after the race. This is a race where legends are made, friends regroup and cultures combine.

Why is the Dakar Rally so unique?

The competitors are placed in a unique, yet complex situation. At any moment during the race, they must mutually support each other, whether it is finding the right direction or fixing a bike or car in the middle of Africa. The rally attracts competitors from all genres of racing; for example, Jacky Ickx came from formula one racing, Robby Gordon from NASCAR, Gaston Rahier and Danny Laporte were both world champions in motocross.

Prominent world political figures such as Ari Vatanen (a member of the European Parliament), Mark Thatcher (son of former British Prime Minister Margaret Thatcher) and Sindiely Wade (daughter of Abdoulaye Wade, current president of Senegal) have all competed in the Dakar Rally.

The Dakar Rally demands preparation on many levels: physically, technically and morally. About 300 hundred motorcycles, 200 cars and over 50 trucks start this endurance event, and less than fifty percent arrive in Dakar. The difficulty of the race is unparalleled. For example, in 1985 141 motorcycles started in Paris and only 28 arrived in Dakar.

The organizers must convince the authorities of other countries to permit the rally to pass. For example, Guinea was closed to the outside world for more than 20 years until the Dakar Rally came through. It is also a venue for major companies like Volkswagen, BMW and KTM to test their new equipment in real time. Amateur riders can compete in a professional event and the organizers give something back to the villages of Africa. The rally can be so many things, both punishing and rewarding. Most of all, it is a challenge to the human spirit.

Chapter 2

BIKE PREPARATION AND THE ANATOMY OF A RALLY/ADVENTURE MOTORCYCLE

Winning contains an element of chance; a mechanical problem is never by chance.

Photo by Thorsten Flechsig.

The art of rally or adventure riding requires a motorcycle that must endure the entire trip. This may be a two day ride of five hundred miles. In the Dakar Rally, however, the distance is about 7500 miles and the ride continues for many days. A rally like this demands a carefully prepared and well-maintained machine. Luckily, most modern motorcycles are very reliable. In days past, this was not the case.

Since much preparation goes into rally and adventure bikes, a basic understanding of the motorcycle is essential. Knowing how to change the oil, fix gear shift levers, deal with mechanical problems and change tires are prerequisite to competing in any event. Inspect the bike before each ride. Know how the bike should feel and know your environment.

Differences between a rally and adventure bike

A rally bike differs from an adventure bike in many ways. A rally bike is a very technical racing machine designed to withstand the harshest of environments for extended periods of time. An adventure bike has many of the same qualities but without some of the performance features. Note that the rally motorcycle discussed here is the KTM rally motorcycle prepared for the Dakar Rally. Other manufacturers prepare their motorcycles much in the same fashion.

• The frame on rally and adventure motorcycles is made

The anatomy of a KTM rally motorcycle. (Photo by Thomas McDonald.)

of Chromium Molybdenum (Chromemoly) with an aluminum sub-frame. Frames are modified for the harsh conditions of rally racing.

• Rally engines have an increased oil capacity to deal with the sustained harsh temperatures experienced during a rally. They have a top speed of about 120 mph (200 km/hr).

• The triple clamps are stronger and the steering head is optimally designed for increased stability and handling which reduces rider fatigue.

• The suspension is tested and modified to accommodate a wide range of conditions. The bike must be supple enough for the rocks and cross grain typically encountered in Morocco, yet progressive enough to handle the G outs and traps encountered in the later stages of the rally.

• The wheels often contain mousses instead of inner tubes for increased reliability.

• The skid plate is made from carbon fiber and contains a two liter water reservoir for rider safety.

• The fairings on a rally motorcycle quickly detach and include pockets for extra storage.

• The navigation instruments are highly sophisticated on rally motorcycle. They include two electronic odometers, a GPS unit, an electronic road book and a digital compass.

Some examples of using safety wiring bolts on a rally bike. (Photos by Johnathan Edwards.)

Potential bolts to safety wire

• gear shift bolt
• caliper bolts
• brake pad clips
• drain plug
• counter shaft sprocket bolt
• steering head bolt
• linkage and shock bolts
• engine mount bolts

• Because of the long distances that must be traversed, rally motorcycles feature very large capacity fuel cells in the range of 30 to 40 liters.

Preparing a bike for an adventure ride

Motorcycles bought right off the showroom floor are often

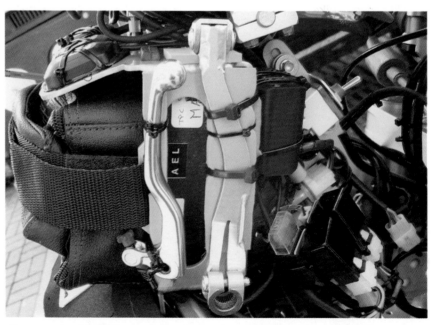

Spare parts should be carried on the motorcycle as much as possible. (Photo by Johnathan Edwards.)

assumed to be ready for toughest of conditions. Experienced mechanics and riders know this is not true.

The basic layout on a rally motorcycle is designed to put the rider in the most comfortable standing position possible. Believe it or not, top rally racers stand on their motorcycles for the majority of the day. It is extremely important to have the handle bar position, foot peg location, seat height and controls adjusted so as to reduce rider fatigue while standing. This cannot be over emphasized.

One's ability to ride a motorcycle at high speeds over unfamiliar terrain is directly linked to one's ability to control the motorcycle in a standing position. This will be covered later in adventure riding techniques.

If you are considering modifying your bike to take part in a long adventure ride or the Dakar Rally, here are some changes you need to consider from the KTM Red Bull rally team mechanics.

Handle bars and grips

As most riding is done in the standing position, Scot Harden advises that you set the handlebars in a position that feels comfortable when you are standing. This position will decrease rider fatigue and maximize control. Handlebar bends are chosen based on the

Most riders use foam grips during the Dakar Rally to decrease hand soreness due to vibration. (Photo by H. Peuker.)

rider preference and comfort. The grips are very important on a rally bike. If you are going on short adventure rides, then just about any handlebar grip will work. However, for long events such as the Dakar Rally, foam grips are the answer. They are

comfortable, decrease hand blisters, and decrease vibration from the long days on the motorcycle. Foam grips can be found in most bicycle shops and are traditionally made for BMX bicycles.

General bike maintenance

One must follow sound mechanical fundamental bike maintenance and stick to the basics. Fix small problems before they become big ones. Check to make sure all bolts are tight. Be sure there are no fluid leaks—radiator, engine oil, and brake fluid. Check for wear on all wiring and hoses and that they are properly isolated.

Developing a daily maintenance schedule is highly critical in a rally or adventure event. (Photo by Thorsten Flechsig.)

Be sure your fanny pack contains the necessary tools for roadside repairs. (Photo by Stephan Legrand.)

Amateurs have it especially tough; they must perform all bike maintenance themselves as well as ride. (Photo by Johnathan Edwards.)

Inspect high wear items frequently—chain, sprockets, brake pads, and tires. Remember, fresh air filters and uncontaminated oil are the lifeblood/lifeline of a motorcycle.

Here is an example that illustrates the importance of bike maintenance: Larry Roseler was competing in the 2004 Dakar Rally. About half way into the rally, Larry was breaking into the top ten in the overall classification. However, he crashed very hard in a sand wash when his front brake caliper bolts fell off. He managed to not injure himself and he brought the bike to the end of the stage. Several people witnessed that his mechanic had properly tightened the bolts the night before, going to show that even the most vigilant of mechanics cannot prepare for everything on the Dakar Rally. The lesson here is to safety wire the bolts.

Consider changing your own engine oil and filters and be familiar how to apply Locktite™ to bolts and screws that may vibrate loose. Adventure rides and the Dakar Rally consist of hundreds, if not thousands of miles. Consider safety wiring essential bolts that would ruin your day if they were to loosen or come off. The counter shaft bolt is a critical one to safety wire because it is under a lot of torque for extended periods of time. Also consider bolts and nuts such as the front brake caliper bolts and oil drain bolt. Your engine mounts bolts could loosen; be sure to wire the nuts in place to avoid losing the motor in the middle of the desert.

Navigation and communication equipment

Navigation equipment usually consists of a GPS (Global Positioning System), odometer and road book and are valuable to any adventure ride or rally. They help keep you on the correct trail, prevent you from getting lost, and may even save your life. It is crucial to be sure all pieces of navigation equipment are mounted in such a way that they are easy to read and still maintain focus on the trail ahead. Riding with navigation equipment is multi tasking in its

The road book and GPS are valuable navigation tools during rally and adventure rides. (Photo by Stephan Legrand.)

highest form; one must learn to shift one's attention from the trail to navigation without compromise for safety.

GPS is the modern day road book; it is a very powerful tool for navigation. The GPS is a satellite-based navigation system made up of a network of 24 satellites placed into orbit by the U.S. Department of Defense. GPS was originally intended for military applications, but in the 1980s, the government made the system available to civilian use. GPS works in all weather conditions, anywhere in the world, twenty-four hours a day.

Many different GPS units are available; use one that is capable of being mounted on a motorcycle. Be careful with GPS units as they often fall off the motorcycle and are difficult to find and

expensive to replace. Learning how to navigate with a GPS unit will be discussed later.

The odometer is an important piece of equipment. Its accuracy is the key to following the road book. Stock odometers are often not accurate and may malfunction easily, usually because of the magnet. The best odometers on the market are electronic odometers. Remember, at best odometers have about a seven percent error. Competitors in the Dakar Rally are required to use electronic odometers.

Fuel capacity

Most adventure motor-cycles need additional fuel capacity; motorcycles in the Dakar Rally must be able to cover a range of 250 kilometers (about 150 miles). Rally bikes have front and rear fuel tanks, increasing the weight of the motorcycle to over 400 pounds when full. Many manufacturers make oversize fuel tanks such as IMS and Acerbis. Depending on the adventure ride, a range of 100 miles is adequate. A range of 200 miles is ideal.

Tires and tubes

Always use ultra heavy duty inner tubes. The stock inner tubes are usually very thin and puncture easily, but they are ideal to carry as spares because they are light weight. Ideally, carry both 18 and 21 inch inner

Rally/adventure tires are made to handle long distances and the increased weight of a rally bike. (Photo courtesy of Dunlop Tire Corporation.)

tubes on long rides. Remember, in emergencies, a 21 inch inner tube can be used to fix both front and rear flats. Also, mousse inserts may be used; however, they are more difficult to change. Upgrade to heavy duty tires. For off-road riding, the new Dunlop 908 rally raid tires are among the best available, providing good traction and durability. Regular motocross tires do not work because the side walls are not strong enough to support the increased weight of the motorcycle; also, heavy duty tires are better because you are going to hit rocks.

Fenders

Most rally bikes come with low lying fenders as you may see on the Dakar Rally. These fenders are great for the road and dry trails and provide more

Tricks from the trade—Scot Harden uses the kickstand to break the bead on a 5 inch rim. (Photo by Johnathan Edwards.)

Low lying fenders are good in dry conditions but poor in muddy conditions. (Photo by Johnathan Edwards.)

airflow to the radiators. In muddy conditions, replace the low lying fenders with traditional high riding fenders because mud will collect under low lying fenders and tear them off. If you unexpectedly encounter mud and have a low lying fender, stop and take it off and strap it to the back fender.

Lights

Being able to see at night is absolutely crucial to rally and adventure riding. Most stock lighting systems meet minimum DOT standards. A wide range of after market options exist that greatly enhance the lighting capacity of the motorcycle.

High Intensity Discharge (HID) lighting systems may increase your margin of safety while riding at night. This is the same technology used on cars and motorcycles in the Baja 1000 which runs well into the night. Baja designs or PIAA offers HID lighting systems for motorcycles. HID battery packs for helmet lighting systems have been introduced recently. The leaders in this field is Baja Designs.

Most stock motorcycles come with plastic reflectors for the headlights. Replace the plastic for glass for better illumination at night. If you ride at night, consider increasing the wattage of the light bulb;

however, be sure the motorcycle produces the appropriate voltage for the light bulb you are installing. The voltage output becomes especially important when you have the GPS and other devices connected to the battery. Take your bike to a shop that knows about modifying lights for off-road riding.

Suspension

Rally and adventure motorcycles have very unique suspension requirements due to the weight and power these motorcycles possess. Most standard adventure motorcycles come with settings more suited to street riding; in most cases, valving and spring rates must be substantially increased. Set the sag in accordance to your height and weight. Also, change the oil in both the forks and shocks because metal particles are in the oil when the shock is new.

The ideal suspension setting should be one that allows for optimal control and compliance in rocks and cross grain situations, while progressive enough to absorb large hits and resist bottoming. Modifying the suspension is different for off-road riding than for motocross; find a suspension tuner who knows off-road riding and your particular brand of motorcycle. Once the suspension is done, it usually does not need to be repeated.

Chapter 3

RIDING GEAR— HOW TO BATTLE THE ELEMENTS

The element of fun always includes danger, to some extent.

Photo by Maindruphoto.

Adventure riding is a lifetime of fun, but with the enjoyment comes an element of danger. Fortunately, the risk of injury can be moderated by using appropriate equipment. In fact, the evolution of riding gear since the days of jeans and boots has been tremendous.

When choosing motorcycle protective gear, comfort is the key for long-distance riding. A general rule is to buy gear that offers superior protection to areas of the body where the bone is just below the surface of the skin e.g. knuckles, shoulders, hips, knees and ankles. Today, enduro gear is widely used, as adventure riding involves both road and off-road.

Helmet

The helmet is the most important protection you will ever invest in. Helmets are designed to absorb shock so that it is not transmitted to your brain. Without a helmet, the shock incurred in a fall, often leads to irreversible brain damage and even death. According to the National Center for Statistics and Analysis, since 2001 over 3000 motorcyclists have died each year in accidents. Over half of these victims were not wearing

Most adventure riders use traditional off-road helmets, but other types work just as well. (Photo by Johnathan Edwards.)

helmets. The percentage of motorcyclists who survive accidents only to be left with brain injury is even higher. Hopefully, you realize the importance of helmets.

The helmet should fit snugly but comfortably as you will be wearing it for extended periods of time. Style of riding and the proportion of road versus dirt, will dictate what kind of helmet you should choose. Most adventure riders and rally racers use traditional off-road helmets, as they are light and agile.

Helmets exist with removable visors, sun screens, radio systems and so on. Consider a helmet with a removable liner, as sweat and grime build up quickly. Helmets also have a definite time frame for which they are effective in preventing a head injury. Read the manufacturer's recommendation to learn about your helmet and replace it when necessary.

Ear Plugs

Wearing ear plugs on long rides is essential. Wind noise and the constant vibration of the motor will cause hearing damage over long periods of time; e.g. tinnitus (a constant ringing in the ears). Keep it simple and use disposable earplugs. Custom fitted ones are available.

Rally jacket

Rally jackets are one of the more essential pieces of equipment next to the helmet. A riding jacket serves many purposes including storage, fluid hydration system, warmth, and protection of the torso, back and upper extremities from rain, rocks and heat. Many jackets are made from Gortex™ material, which helps to prevent moisture build-up and keeps the body warm. Many jackets will convert into a vest by removing

Always keep a rain jacket in case of unforeseen weather. (Photo by H. Mitterbauer.)

Next to a helmet, a rally jacket is one of the most important pieces of riding gear. (Photo by H. Mitterbauer.)

the sleeves. Jackets should also have a lot of storage for parts, food and maps. Manufacturers like Fox, MSR, and KTM Hard Equipment all make rally jackets.

Boots

Riding boots are very important. They must be durable enough to stabilize the ankle, rigid enough to deflect rocks and yet comfortable enough to wear all day long. If you are going to be riding in wet weather, consider boots that have a waterproof inner layer (e.g. Gortex™) which not only offers protection from rain but also provides warmth. Consider the new generation of boots with synthetic construction as they dry a lot quicker.

Socks reduce skin chaffing from the boot. Choose socks based on the conditions you are riding in. If you are riding in neutral conditions, cotton socks may be adequate. If you are going to be wet or in high temperatures, choose socks

KTM Red Bull rider Chris Blais uses wool socks along with Dr. Scholl's shoe liners during the Dakar Rally. (Photo by DPPI.)

made of Gortex™ or polypropylene, because they prevent moisture build up on your skin.

Riding pants

Riding pants, formerly called leathers, are designed to protect the skin, provide air flow and to hold knee protectors. There is no one riding pant that delivers everything, such as cool in summer, warm in winter, waterproof and quick drying, with crash and slide protection. Many different styles and brands exist. Some are designed better for off-road riding than others.

Many miles on a motorcycle often leads to chaffed bottoms. Prevention will avoid a skin rash or breakdown. Keep your skin dry with application of baby powder or a similar product. Use quality underpants with padding or cycling shorts. Troy Lee Designs makes a padded short which is good for long distance riding.

Knee braces

Knee braces are intended to prevent injury by limiting extension, side to side mobility and protection of the patella. Many riders use them to prevent knee injuries even if they have never had one. If you have laxity of the knee ligaments, then you may need them; consult a sports medicine physician about this subject. Knee braces are expensive and range from around two hundred to more than seven hundred dollars. Before investing in knee braces ask your friends about their experiences. Be sure to choose knee braces which do not tear through your riding pants.

Kidney belts

Riding long distances over rough terrain and motor vibration stress your inner organs and back. Kidney belts are designed to minimize your inner organs (e.g. spleen, liver and kidneys) from bouncing as well as provide some support to the lower back. Most motorcycle gear manufacturers or sporting goods stores carry kidney belts.

Goggles

Goggles protect your eyes from flying debris, dirt, rocks, sticks, bugs, cold, heat and

Goggles come in many different styles, choose the one for the weather conditions you are riding in. (Photo by by Johnathan Edwards.)

fumes. Appropriate goggle selection includes comfort, peripheral vision, adaptability to roll off systems and whether they can be worn with prescription glasses.

Remember all lens have some amount of distortion built into them due to the curvature when they are fitted into the goggle frame; some lenses have more distortion than others. Thus it is very important to try as many different types of lenses as possible to compare and contrast the amount of distortion. Distortion becomes even more of a factor with age and as your eyesight changes. Through trial and error, you will find the correct lens.

Weather conditions and the amount of sun light can have an effect on lens selection. For example, in the Dakar Rally, Morocco is often overcast and most riders choose orange or yellow lens, in contrast to Mauritania where the sun is often blazing and riders often choose dark or clear lens.

Anti-fog capability is valuable in any goggle system.

Lens that allow air flow, such as double pane lens, will decrease fog. Also anti-fog cloths help prevent fogging. Products like Rain-X helps rain to bead off the lens for extended periods of time. You can obtain Rain-X from most auto parts stores. Dust repellent works by spraying a chemical on both sides of the lens.

Wearing a head cap or bandanna can decrease the amount of sweat that travels from your helmet to your goggles. Goggles are useless if you can not see. In adverse conditions, which can appear at any time during an adventure ride or rally, tear offs and roll offs can be essential. A tear off clears the entire field of vision because the removable clear film lies over the entire lens; roll offs are a 1/4 inch strip of clear film, parallel with the eyes, which clears the field of vision with the pull of a string.

If you wear prescription glasses, a company called Pro-Vue (*vue* meaning sight in French) constructs goggles to fit a variety of prescription glasses.

Gloves

Maximum protection is needed for the hands as the skin around the fingers and knuckles is thin and does not heal easily. You also need protection against the cold weather. Cold hands do not give your brain the feedback it needs to control things like hard braking. Conversely, desert riding in thick warm gloves can be frustrating in the heat.

We all prefer a particular brand of gloves; for some unknown reason, some gloves fit our hands better than others. For example, if you are a physician, you do not want to return to work after a weekend adventure ride with huge hand blisters. Gloves should fit well, allowing a certain degree of freedom while protecting your knuckles from flying rocks. Also, consider Gortex™ gloves for riding in cold weather. When buying gloves, it is true that you get what you pay for. Shop around and consider glove liners if necessary.

Taping

A common practice by many top racers is taping. Taping the hand provides the skin an additional layer of protection against blisters. Many

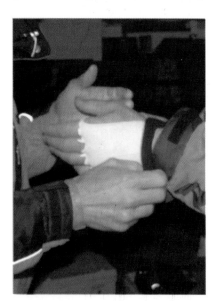

Taping the hand is excellent for preventing blisters. (Photo by Johnathan Edwards.)

different ways exist to tape the hands; it is very important that taping be done in such a way that the tape does not ball up in the palm, further increasing the chances of blisters. Additionally, the taping should not be so restrictive that it limits hand movement and circulation.

Chest protector

Chest protectors help prevent injury from rocks and crashes. When the ride involves different terrains, including rocks, ruts, and the like, a chest protector may prevent injury to your collar bone and even the internal organs such as your spleen and liver. Chest protectors may be worn on the outside or inside of the riding jersey. The top of the line rally jackets usually incorporate

some type of shoulder, back and forearm protection in lieu of a traditional chest protector. Acerbis even makes a chest protector designed for women.

Fanny packs

The tools and parts you carry in a fanny pack may be the only means to arrive at the next

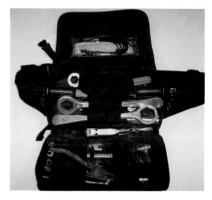

The tools in a fanny pack should allow for most trailside repairs. (Photo by Johnathan Edwards.)

Getting wet is part of the ride, so prepare by having the proper gear in advance. (Photo by Maindruphoto.)

check point or camp. The tools selected should allow for most trailside repairs. Combination wrenches save weight and space. Many companies such as Motion Pro design tools specifically for fanny packs. Essential items one may carry in a fanny pack include bolts and nuts, CO_2 canisters, money, tape, tire irons, tools, tube, zip-ties and food.

How to prepare for cold weather and heat

When the sun stops shining or temperatures rise above what you are used to and you decide to go riding anyway, prepare for the elements. Layer your clothes properly. The first layer should be a polypropylene or capilene shirt and underpants. This way moisture is drawn away from the skin. Never use cotton as it retains moisture and feels miserable when it gets damp. Gortex™ makes a good exterior layer because it prevents water from getting to your skin as well as allowing sweat to pass through.

Adventure riding usually involves cold weather and surviving the elements. Always be prepared by checking weather conditions before leaving. Creating and maintaining waterproofing of boots, jackets, gloves and tents is a complex subject. However, start with extra clothing and strip down as necessary. Carry extra clothes in your backpack for wet conditions such as an extra pair of gloves. In desperate situations remember many convenience stores carry work gloves. Consider using an electric heated vest or jacket liner. Many riders use them in the Atlas mountains of Morocco during the Rally.

In extreme cold weather, the goal is to prevent hypothermia. Take whatever action necessary to keep your body warm as the consequences of hypothermia can be catastrophic. An extreme example is that frostbite can occur in susceptible areas in less than fifteen minutes when riding in winds of 80 to 90 mph and 0 degrees Fahrenheit. This is not hard to do when riding fast on a motorcycle.

Chapter 4

MOTHER NATURE & THE ADVENTURE RIDER

Ride knowing the unforeseen is always out there.

Photo by Stephan Legrand.

Mother Nature is the joy and pain of rally and adventure riders. It is nature's beauty with sunsets, mountains and oceans that takes our breath away and gives us inspiration to ride. Mother Nature also provides challenging obstacles for the rally rider which require skill as well as instinct. Challenges of the outdoors defines rally riding for each of these obstacles— trees, rocks, water crossings, sand dunes and camel grass—a knowledge of how to maneuver the motorcycle through them can make all the difference.

Having the confidence to control a rally bike over various terrains is something gained by experience and learning from others. (Photo by Jonathan Beck.)

Trees

Trees come in many forms. Standing, lying, hanging, large and small, they tend not to be very forgiving obstacles. First and foremost, do not hurt the tree and it will not hurt you. You may encounter them crossing Death Valley or at ten thousand feet in the Atlas Mountains of Morocco. Riding around trees requires patience and going slow. Adventure rides are too long to blast through trees. Hand guards are a must and consider using elbow pads, especially if you have previous injuries. Ride with your elbows and knees tucked in, and keep the toes pointed forward to avoid snagging them on anything.

Tree roots can take a motorcycle down in a milli-

19

second. Remember that tree roots are often exposed close to the tree, so be prepared. If you see a patch of leaves, assume a root is under them; likewise, behind every bush is a rock. Stand up if possible when riding in roots, as the front and rear tires can suddenly give away, especially if the tire contacts the root at an angle. Always use mousse inner tubes or run heavy duty inner tubes and carry extras. Safety wiring the rear brake and gear shifter will help them from getting damaged.

Rocks

Rocks are tough on both the rider and motorcycle; part of being a good rider is taking care of the bike. "One must make it to the pink lake to finish" is a common Dakar Rally proverb. Rocks are common obstacles on the Dakar Rally and on adventure rides. Some different situations that arise are rock beds, boulders, small rocks on fast roads, as well as rock formations.

Muscling a rally bike through rocks is asking for trouble; riding tense in the rocks increases the chances of falling. Let the bike work beneath you, using your legs to control the direction of the bike. Think of going through rocks like a chess game, your move is to ride in a centered position using finesse and maintaining enough momentum to get over a rock, but moving slow enough to be

The basics of riding through rocks are to use the legs to control the bike and steady throttle control to manage the bike forward. (Photo by G. Soldano.)

able to stop on a dime to stay out of trouble. Many injuries to the feet occur when riding through rocks. Keep the feet pointed straight or raise them above the rocks. Often feet and ankles are injured by rocks that were never seen.

Mousse inner tubes have revolutionized riding through rocks. Before mousse inner tubes, one had to avoid hitting rocks for fear of puncturing the tube. Nowadays, mousse inner tubes allow one to hit rocks straight on. There are pros and cons to hitting rocks straight on. The pros are not having to turn the bike unnecessarily to avoid the rocks. This allows the rider to take a straighter line, saving time by hitting rocks straight on. Speed can be maintained and

there is less risk of flat tire. The cons of running mousse inner tubes include overconfidence gained by hitting rocks straight on and the increased chance of falling, causing damage to bike and body.

Camel grass

Riding through camel grass is akin to riding through unevenly spaced, sharp, hard, 3-foot whoops. Often, the rider must weave through these randomly placed mini-dunes with hard centers. Camel grass is a sheer test of patience and endurance; competitors endured three hours of camel grass in a single stage during the 2005 rally. Riding smoothly and consistently is the key to

2006 Dakar Rally champion, Marc Coma patiently works his way through a section of camel grass in Mauritania. (Photo by DPPI.)

Walking across a river may be the way to cross, especially if there are a lot of rocks or you cannot see the bottom. (Photo by G. Soldano.)

overcoming camel grass. How much energy you conserve depends on your speed and the lines you choose.

Water crossings

Water crossings are one of the most elusive of the obstacles Mother Nature likes to challenge us. The depth of the water, what lies at the bottom and the speed of the current are all variables to be considered. A popular Dakar Rally story is about a well known Spanish rider named Jordi Acarons. He had a sizeable lead in the Dakar Rally when he crossed a river in Senegal. He misjudged the depth and fell, and water entered the engine. The rest sputtered into history.

As a general rule, do not cross a river unless you can see the bottom or you see someone

Crossing rivers can be challenging. Here, Giovani Sala takes his time through the water. (Photo by G. Soldano.)

else cross first. Cross a stream at the sides because objects tend to be in the center and it is deeper. Be sure the electrical system and air box are sealed. If water enters your electrical

system, you will usually have to wait until it dries and then try to start the bike. The current of a river or stream is often underestimated. Consider walking across the river first and be sure to assess the current by tossing a stick or leaf and watching its speed downstream. When you do cross the river, take the most direct route, stand up, and center your weight. If there are a lot of rocks, walk it across. If possible, ride with your feet up so they do not get soaked, because blisters will form if you continue the day riding with wet socks and boots.

Climbs

Climbing a hill on a rally motorcycle is much different than on an enduro motorcycle. As agile as the rally bike may

Chris Blais climbs this rocky uphill maintaining the attack position. (Photo by DPPI.)

KTM Red Bull Rally Team
Tips to
Climbing Hills

- Evaluate the climb first
- Stand up
- Lean forward slightly
- Commit fully
- Maintain constant throttle control

Blais advises that once you start the climb, you must be fully committed. However, if you do not feel confident about a climb, then find another way around. Abandoning or bailing out of a climb is more difficult on a rally bike due to the weight.

To illustrate the challenges of hill climbs, one of the KTM Dakar riders was training in southern Nevada, just after a rain storm. As he approached a rocky uphill, he became stuck and had to pick up the bike around fifteen times because of slippery rocks. His heart rate maxed out to the 190's and his riding gear was soaked from sweating profusely—a very bad situation that could compromise one's ability to finish a rally or ride. Keep in mind the normal rally bike weighs around 350 to 450 pounds.

A 640 KTM Adventure motorcycle has enough power to climb just about any hill. Be sure to look at the hill first and pick a line without obstacles. If you hit rocks, ruts, and trees, this will throw the rhythm of the climb off and you may have to

Reaching the top of a dune requires much skill. Always maintain enough momentum to reach the crest of the dune. (Photo by Scott Cox.)

be, it weighs 350 – 450 pounds (150 – 200 kg). Throwing a rally bike away on a climb may damage the motorcycle (and rider) more than with a smaller motorcycle.

Scot Harden always tells his students to stand up on the motorcycle during the climb. "If you are sitting down, you are merely a passenger." Factory KTM Red Bull rally racer Chris start again on the middle of the hill. Try to get a run up the hill standing up, keeping the motorcycle straight and maintaining the attack position. Maintain a constant RPM going up the hill for the best traction. Remember that you may have to compensate for unexpected rocks or ruts. Try not to follow other riders up a climb; you will be stuck right behind them.

Nonetheless, bailing out of a climb is a necessary evil. Once you realize that you will not make the climb, the best thing to do is to stop, apply both brakes, then lean the bike over toward the hill and position the bike perpendicular to the trail. Then decide if you can continue up from there or go down the hill and give it another attempt.

Down hills

Descending a hill can be as difficult as the way up. The same principles apply as

Careful planning is the key to negotiating tough down hills. Choose the smoothest line and use finesse to reach the bottom. (Photos by Jonathan Beck.)

climbing with the addition of using the brakes. Choose a good line, descend at a comfortable speed, stand up, look ahead and use your front brake. Controlling the motorcycle down a hill is done with the front brake. The rear brake may help if used sparingly, but do not lock it up and start sliding.

Baked mud

When the sun dries out wet dirt, a caked dirt surface appears which is cracked and breaks apart easily. Be aware when riding on baked mud because traction may be compromised and slide outs are more common. Ride baked mud carefully; be watchful on dry lake beds and after rains.

Barbed wire

Barbed wire is encountered on many adventure rides, usually around farms, property lines and fences; it is often placed carelessly. Barbed wire causes

2005 Dakar champion Cyril Despres descends this trail in perfect form, standing up and slightly back on the motorcycle. (Photo by DPPI.)

Barbed wire and other foreign objects can create serious problems on the trail. Always carry wire cutters and pliers for such emergencies. (Photo by Johnathan Edwards.)

flats, gets caught up in sprockets, causes wheels to lock up and it may even cause injury. Be aware of your surroundings and if you have barbed wire in the wheel, stop immediately and remove it with the wire cutters in your fanny pack. Scot Harden was racing in the desert and barbed wire consumed his rear wheel. He recalls that had he not taken his wire cutters that day, his race would have been a complete failure. Always carry a pair of wire cutters.

Bushes and cactus

Remember to treat every bush as if there was a rock in or behind it. Bushes can also be like miniature trees, throwing you off and even damaging the bike. Avoid bushes whenever possible.

There are many types of cactus in the desert. Most cacti have thorns which can be difficult to remove. Never hit a cactus, because some types will release their branches, and you and the bike will be covered in cactus thorns. Use pliers or strong tweezers to remove the thorns and do not wait, just get it over with.

Dust

Riding in dust is a reality of off-road riding. Most dislike dust with a passion, but some riders truly have a talent for it. Riding in dust is inefficient and you need to be able to change lines

if you want a chance around the rider in front of you. If you cannot see in the dust, slow down or stop, move to a safer line and then continue. Scot Harden advises against following riders too long in the

dust as you may ruin the air filter and increase the chance of a crash. Dust will only slow you down, and thus in a race, he advises to do whatever possible to pass a rider who is dusting him out. Watch the bike in front

The stillness of the morning creates a situation where dust hangs for several minutes. This is one of the most challenging aspects of riding in dust. (Photo by DPPI.)

Dust and sand storms can be very intense during the Dakar rally. (Photo by Johnathan Edwards.)

of you, as this may allow you to miss or slow down for obstacles that the bike in front has hit.

Fog

Fog is another visual impairment that is often dealt with in the Dakar Rally. Usually in Morocco, many mornings will have fog and everyone has to go slow. Ride with extreme caution because the risk of hitting another rider or an object is very high.

Animals

In any type of adventure ride or rally, animals are often present. Avoiding animals is the best policy; always be on the defensive when riding close to them. Many different types of animals are encountered on the Dakar Rally: birds, burros, camels, cows, dogs, goats and

Camels and motorcycles traverse the same terrain. (Photo by Maindruphoto.)

Animals like these camels and monkeys are a common sight throughout the Dakar rally. (Photos by Johnathan Edwards and Thomas McDonald.)

Alfie Cox demonstrates that mules are encountered just about everywhere in Africa. (Photo by H. Peuker.)

Ride carefully through cattle herds. (Photo by Stephan Legrand.)

monkeys. Riders often encounter packs of monkeys, especially in Mali and Senegal. Burros often will not move for anything as they do not see well. While driving in the Dakar Rally, a KTM mechanic ran over a burro in Mauritania and felt horrible about the situation. In an instance like this, one has to be careful because, regardless of country, native people may call the police, even if it may have been an accident. Consider offering payment on the spot if confronted.

Always be aware of dead animals in the road. They often lay in the middle of the road and can be a serious obstacle.

Mine shafts

Mine shafts exist in many parts of the California, Nevada and Utah deserts. There is wonderful riding all around abandoned mines, but pay special attention as many are abandoned and not marked. Also, mine shafts may appear suddenly at the top of a climb. To say the least, falling into a mineshaft may ruin your day.

Loam

Loam is soft soil which normally provides excellent traction. However, a sense of overconfidence can be felt riding loam dirt sections, especially on a heavy rally bike. One may experience the rear end of the motorcycle moving side to side when traveling at high speeds; dragging the rear brake may stabilize the rear wheel in this situation.

Mud

Riding a rally bike in the mud can be quite a challenge since it is heavier than most motorcycles. Mud often sticks to the bike, causing mechanical issues and increased wear. Watch out when using low lying front fenders. Mud will collect under the fender and tear it off very quickly. If you suspect that you will hit mud during the trip, install a high riding fender, like that found on an enduro bike. One can also consider spraying silicone on the bottom of the fenders to prevent mud from collecting. Ride more conservatively in mud, as picking up a rally bike in the mud

2005 Dakar champion Cyril Despres is first to cross through this section of mud. (Photo by G. Soldano.)

can be a chore that requires two or more persons. Choose outside lines to maintain momentum and to decrease the chance of sliding out.

Sand

An entire book can be written about riding in sand. The next chapter in this book has a whole section devoted to this subject. The difficulties of sand riding are instability, maintaining momentum, working the engine harder and using more gas than one would otherwise expect.

Wind

Riding in the wind has both its pros and cons; it difficult to control the motorcycle, but it can be a godsend if it clears the dust as you approach upcoming riders. If you feel the bike becoming less stable while you are experiencing a strong gust, slow down as this will increase stability.

Setting a pace

If you are an amateur or just trying out adventure riding in a school, maintain a safe pace for your skill level. Trying to keep up with the others is a recipe for disaster. Learn at your own pace; chances are that you have a job to return to Monday morning. There is no shame in making others wait for you but there is shame in taking their time while they call for medical

Maintaining a safe pace through difficult terrain comes from sound, fundamental techniques. (Photo by Johnathan Edwards.)

assistance to transport you to the hospital.

Passing other riders

Passing other riders in a rally or adventure ride can be challenging. On one hand, do not be over aggressive, because the adventure ride is not a race. It is about the experience of the whole group, not just a single rider. When passing a colleague, be sure about the line and pass you are executing, and keep in mind the skill level of other riders. If a rider goes down when you pass, more time is wasted cleaning up the mess than if you had just waited until the correct moment.

Adverse events

Getting lost is a part of adventure riding. One story of being lost during the Dakar Rally comes from Serge Bacou

(who finished second overall in the motorcycles division, 1988). "I have two bad memories of the Dakar Rally. In 1986 I broke my leg, and in 1982 I was lost for three days and three nights, alone, without a beacon, without water, with nothing to eat and it was minus 5 degrees Celsius (23° F) at night. This experience was horrible, but enriching at the same time. I still feel the memories when I come to the desert."

In 1982, Mark Thatcher, son of then-British Prime Minister Margaret Thatcher, along with his French co-driver Charlotte Verney and their mechanic, went missing for six days. On January 9th, the trio became separated from a convoy of vehicles after they stopped to make repairs to a faulty steering arm. They were declared missing on January 12; after a large-scale search, a C130 Hercules search plane

from the Algerian military spotted their white Peugeot some 50 km off course. Thatcher, Verney and the mechanic were all unharmed.

Stories like these are the very reason why we use GPS and road books to navigate terrain. If you are lost, do not panic. Follow someone if you are lost; at least you will be lost with someone else. Be sure you have a fanny pack of tools and extra food and water. If you are lost, seek higher ground and search for points of reference. Use the GPS as a compass. A real compass, however, is always good backup in case the GPS malfunctions, batteries die or there is no satellite reception. Remember, the sun rises in east and sets in the west. Think through the situation and usually your first instinct is correct.

If you are separated from the group because of a fall or mechanical problems, stay in one place or go back to a point you are certain of, so that someone can backtrack and find you. Never ride alone and use satellite phones if possible. Nowadays, these phones are smaller, more affordable, and can save your life. KTM Red Bull factory rider, Kellon Walch, fell in the Baja Mexican desert while pre-running for the San Felipe 250. Using a satellite phone, the people helping Kellon were able to communicate with the KTM team physician and receive medical advice.

Chapter 5

ADVENTURE RIDING TECHNIQUES

Things should be made as simple as possible, but not any simpler ~ Albert Einstein

Photo by Jean Aignan Museau.

Becoming a good motorcycle rider requires much time and practice; how we practice forever shapes our riding style. Before delving into certain riding techniques, one thing is evident in the world of motorcycling: we buy the bikes and walk out the door. We are left to trial and error to learn how to ride the motorcycle and this often leads to unnecessary injury. Team sports like football, baseball and soccer have set a foundation for designated practices under the supervision of a coach whose job it is to watch and critique each player. This foundation is rare in most facets of motorcycling; schools for learning advanced techniques exist; however, they are not easily accessible. Participating in a school will improve riding skills, decrease injuries and increase the enjoyment of the riding experience.

Rally and adventure riding entail both on- and off-road riding skills. For example, learning how to control a motorcycle in the dirt can be life saving on the asphalt. Thus, we recommend learning the basics on the dirt, starting very simple and then applying those skills.

The essence of learning and appreciating adventure riding is to keep things simple and build a solid foundation.

Standing up

Standing up on the motorcycle is one of the most important principles you will

Adventure riding camps are a valuable tool for improving skills. (Photo by Stephan Legrand.)

Standing up through fast corners maintains control and speed as the Spanish rider Marc Coma demonstrates. (Photo by H. Peuker.)

learn to control a motorcycle over any type of terrain. As discussed in chapter 2, set up your bike so that you are comfortable riding in the standing position. Notice that motocross, enduro and trials riders always attack technical sections standing on their foot pegs. The standing position actually lowers the center of gravity by directing weight over the foot pegs

making the motorcycle more stable. You can also see better when standing up. Practice standing on the motorcycle until it becomes second nature.

Another valuable technique is learning to turn a rally bike while standing. You will gain more control and confidence if you practice standing up through tight corners (barrel turns, for

example) that you would normally sit down for.

Turns

Look for the simple things in turns you understand well, recognize a pattern in those simple things and then use that pattern and apply it to more complicated turns. Many schools start out by practicing turns; one exercise is barrel

(Photos by Johnathan Edwards.)

1. Scot Harden shows control entering the corner
 a. Scot is standing in the neutral position, with the elbows up.
 b. The front brake is providing stopping power before the apex of the corner.
 c. The rear brake sets the bike up for the turn.
 d. Note all braking is done before the apex.

2. In the corner
 a. Scot slides forward, transferring his body weight to the front of the bike.
 b. Momentum and inertia carry Scot through the first third of the turn.
 c. Rear wheel is not sliding out, but tracking in the turn.
 d. Inside leg is out and used as a counter balance.

3. Out of the corner
 a. The inside leg is moving back to the foot peg.
 b. Acceleration is smooth and progressive.
 c. Body weight is transferred toward the rear of the bike for maximum traction.
 d. Scot is looking ahead to the next corner.

Accelerate out of corners with rocks standing up and looking ahead to maintain speed. (Photo by G. Soldano.)

Kellon Walch uses his legs to turn the bike while keeping his elbows raised. (Photo by H. Peuker.)

turns. This is a classic example of how to practice something simple and then build from the experience. Everyone has a preference in which way they turn the bike; become accustomed to turning the bike both ways. Practice over and over again with different

Braking and turning a large displacement adventure bike can be intimidating. However, the same principles apply to it as to a motocross bike as Scot Harden demonstrates. (Photo by Jonathan Beck.)

motorcycles in opposite directions. Master the art of this exercise, and you will successfully manage more complicated turns and situations.

Braking and the rally bike

During Scot Harden's rally adventure camps, he asks his riders: "What is the most important mechanism we have for maintaining speed and control?" The answer is the front brake.

Braking is a science, and this is why an entire section is being devoted here to techniques of braking and how it applies to the rally bike and

adventure riding. Fundamentally, braking is an easy concept, but perfection is not easily obtained. Many factors contribute to braking, such as the weight of the bike, size of the discs, speed, terrain, tires and brake pads.

Generally, the front brake contributes about seventy percent of the braking power, while the engine and rear brake contribute the rest. Novice riders hesitate to use the front brake, while more experienced riders use it aggressively. Different than other forms of racing, rally racing usually involves braking from high speeds in order to make a turn or to avoid an obstacle. Applying the front brake transfers the weight of the bike forward, forcing the rider to hold on to the bike tighter and with more force.

Proper body positioning while braking is usually standing with elbows raised and body centered, keeping the bike in a straight forward position. Standing with the elbows raised allows the rider to compensate for bumps or rocks hit during braking. Keeping the bike straight during braking is critical on a rally bike because the bike is heavy and hard to control; sliding sideways at high speeds increases the chances of crashing. Using the front brake during barrel turning drills helps teach these techniques.

Braking should be a smooth and progressive motion. Upon entering the turn, the front forks should drop down smoothly and consistently. They should drop down in one motion, not moving up and down because of hesitation in using the front brake.

Improving the quality of braking on a rally bike is done with special parts and with meticulous maintenance of the brakes. The KTM Red Bull team uses oversize brake discs to improve braking. Bleeding the brakes often, as well as changing brake pads, is important for effective braking. Also, remove oil from the rotors with brake cleaner. Tires make a difference in braking as well; a dual sport tire will not grab as much as a tire with large knobbies. Using the motor to

brake can be a very effective means of slowing down.

Braking is very hard on rally motorcycles because of the weight and speeds achieved. The brakes will heat up very easily and braking power will decrease dramatically; this occurs very frequently in mountainous terrain. If your brakes overheat, ride slow until the brakes come back or consider stopping until they cool down.

Special braking situations

These include push steering, deep sand, off-camber turns, low speed and smooth corners. Push steering is locking up the front and/or rear brakes while steering the motorcycle around an obstacle. It can be life saving when an unexpected object is approached

at high speeds. Deep sand is difficult because momentum must be maintained at the same time while applying the brakes. Practice in sand if possible and consider using the motor as a brake before pulling in the levers to slow down. Off-camber turns require precision braking and must be done with careful consideration. Standing or seated, braking before an off-camber turn is essential as well as positioning the body over the bike to maintain a good center of gravity.

Sand dunes

Sand dunes are a huge challenge for competitors in the Dakar Rally as well as on adventure rides. During the 2005 Dakar Rally one rider said, "There are times when the front wheel just disappears into the

Cyril Despres maintaining his momentum by keeping the throttle on in the deep sand. Always be ready to accelerate out of soft spots. (Photo by H. Peuker.)

Riding the sand dunes in Death Valley—a surreal experience. (Photo by Scott Cox.)

soft sand without warning, stopping the bike and throwing me over the handlebars."

Navigation around sand dunes is often known to be the most difficult of maneuvers because riders are unfamiliar with the terrain as well as the variability of the sand. Sand dunes differ in many parts of the world; in Africa the composition of the sand is much finer, sometimes like powder, whereas the sand in North America is usually much coarser. Also, the sand dunes in Africa may have pockets of ultra soft sand that can instantly swallow a motorcycle. Many injuries occur in sand because it is a very unstable environment and falls are common. Mental and physical fatigue is a factor in sand dunes, especially if riders have to pick up their bikes after falling or getting stuck in the sand. Remember, where there are sand dunes, there is also extreme heat; fluid hydration is paramount.

A sand dune story

American KTM Red Bull factory racer Kellon Walch was leading stage seven of the 2005 Dakar Rally the entire day, until he arrived at the sand dunes. As he approached what looked to be a small sand

The African sand is notorious for swallowing rally bikes. (Photo by David Rauseo.)

2006 Dakar champion Marc Coma correctly rides the crest of this sand dune at an angle. (Photo by H. Peuker.)

KTM Red Bull Rally Team Secrets to Riding Sand

1. Avoid braking in sand, use the engine or rear brake if possible.

2. Maintain momentum.

3. Be ready to accelerate out of soft sand.

4. Approach steep dunes at an angle.

5. Look for others tracks.

6. Never use the front brake in powder like sand.

7. Drag the rear brake to stabilize the back wheel.

8. Ride with a higher gear.

9. Take your time, be consistent.

10. Maintain hydration; take the time to drink.

dune, little did he know a sand bowl was on the other side. Kellon explained that he launched off the sand dune with too much speed, hit the other side of the bowl, and the force of the impact violently separated him from his motorcycle. He then had to dig himself out of the sand, which cost him the stage win. This example demonstrates the unpredictability of sand dunes and how even an expert rider must be careful when approaching even the most innocent looking dunes.

Principles of riding sand dunes

First, when riding in sand dunes assume the sand is soft and maintain momentum; always be ready to accelerate out of soft spots. It is crucial to maintain momentum when climbing sand dunes. Judgment is especially difficult because you cannot see what is on the other side of the dune. Often, the dune may be too steep on the other side, or even worse, you may encounter a sand bowl. Approach steep dunes at an angle, maintaining momentum.

KTM Red Bull rider Chris Blais explains that he always gains just enough momentum with the motorcycle to reach the top of the dune. This technique allows

Approaching steep dunes on an angle allows the rider a view of what lies on the other side. (Photo by Scott Cox.)

you the choice of not getting stuck at the peak of the dune and not being forced to descend a part of the dune that is too steep. Also, many dunes are too soft to approach straight on and may stop the bike suddenly.

When descending the back side of a dune, maintain a little throttle, position yourself back on the bike and stand up on the foot pegs. By riding standing up, you will be ready for sudden decelerations or dropoffs. Some riders find it useful to grip the tank with their legs to avoid being thrown forward in very soft spots.

Efficiency is the key to riding sand dunes. Never ride a sand dune as if it was the last day of the ride or rally. Saving energy is crucial for many reasons. Realize that sand dunes are usually located in very hot deserts. Most riders complain that having to pick up a rally bike in the sand is one of the most physically exhausting exercises they encounter during the Dakar Rally. Often the heart rate reaches a maximum while picking up the bike. Save energy and remember to drink from your hydration system often.

Braking is different in the sand; consider using the engine to slow down before getting on the brakes. Using the brakes in the sand may cost too much momentum and force you to stop or even crash; be very careful using the front brake as you may

Scot Harden demonstrates the importance of maintaining momentum and keeping your weight back while descending dunes. (Photo by Scott Cox.)

find yourself suddenly thrown over the bars. In fact, most expert riders only use the rear brake. Also, many riders encounter swapping of the back wheel in sand; dragging the rear brake helps stabilize the back end of the motorcycle.

Navigating sand dunes can be very complex and mistakes

The size, shape and consistency of the sand dunes make them very hard to ride. (Photo by DPPI.)

are burned out on sand dunes; this is because the rear wheel encounters more resistance and drag on the sand. Also, most riders use a higher gear to get through the sand. As a result, the rider must fan the clutch more than usual and the rear wheel spins approximately two to three times more in the sand than on hard ground. Additionally, expect to use more gas when navigating through sand dunes because it is easy to get lost.

Situations unique to sand dunes

Former factory BMW rider Jimmy Lewis explains very well that African sand dunes are much different than in the U.S.A. and that even the most experienced riders cannot judge where the soft sand will occur. The sand in Africa is finer and more like powder. The fineness of the sand may cause you to sink or even stop the bike instantly, possibly throwing you over the bars. This is why it is so important to maintain momentum through the sand and be ready for soft spots. According to Kellon Walch, the

can cost precious time during a rally. Commonly, a rider approaches a sand dune and the GPS arrow points to a path straight through the dunes. The decision becomes a choice of passing straight through, as this would be the shortest point to the next waypoint, or to take a route around the dunes which is longer in distance but may avoid the difficulty of getting stuck. Preferably, look for other tracks to follow. Otherwise, it may be safer to go around or find the smallest, safest dune crossing.

During the 2006 Dakar Rally, American privateer James Embro explained how he approached a difficult set of dunes in Mauritania. The road book showed the dune crossing to be about 30 kilometers with

GPS waypoints dispersed within. He gauged how much daylight remained and his degree of fatigue, and chose to ride around the dunes. He would receive penalties for missing the waypoints, but he did this because his goal was to finish the Dakar Rally. James' strategy worked and he arrived in Dakar.

Remember sand dunes are very hard on the clutch and use more gas. Many clutches

Danny Laporte flies across the sand in Death Valley at a hundred miles per hour. (Photo by Scott Cox.)

soft spots are usually located around the smaller dunes.

A situation unique to sand dunes is getting stuck and then having to start again. Do not attempt to just accelerate when you are stuck as you will dig the rear wheel deeper into the sand. First, dismount and lean the bike to the side; this allows sand to fall underneath the rear wheel. Then gas it out of the sand while pushing the bike. If you encounter a soft spot, many riders advise to dismount immediately and walk the bike across the sand to avoid being stuck.

Sand bowls can be treacherous and frustrating. Many a rally rider's day has ended in a sand bowl with a helicopter air lifting the motorcycle to the clean up camion. The rider has to use momentum to get out of a bowl, rather than riding straight up the face. Start at the bottom and ride in circles until you have enough momentum to exit the sand bowl. Also, look at the top of the bowl to be sure no one else is coming over the top while you are trying to exit. Again, pay attention to small sand dunes; a sand bowl could be on the other side.

Reading the sand dunes can be a very difficult task. Sand dunes change constantly due to wind, other riders and moisture. Never go straight up and over the peak of a sand dune assuming that you know what the backside is like. Approach sand dunes at an angle so you can look over the other side, then decide whether to descend or not.

High speed straights

Traveling at high speeds on a motorcycle is a natural part of adventure riding and rally

Chris Blais demonstrates the classic high speed attack position. His body is slightly forward and his eyes are scanning. (Photo by H. Peuker.)

racing; speeds around 120 miles per hour are often recorded during the Dakar Rally. The BMW 1200 or KTM Adventure 950 are certainly capable of going faster. High speeds occur on lake beds, dirt roads and even some trails. 2006 Dakar champ Marc Coma says that the high speeds encountered during the rally is one of the biggest differences compared to other types of racing. Scot Harden also notes that multitasking involved in

riding a rally bike requires the highest of vigilance.

Some general rules for riding at high speeds include reading the terrain, using a steering stabilizer, knowing your surroundings, avoiding over-confidence and sudden movements, and riding slightly

back on the bike. Following a consistent set of rules can make the difference between a successful run and a catastrophic crash. Keep in mind that high speeds should only be reserved for experienced riders. The goal during an adventure ride is to finish, so going fast is a second priority.

The motorcycle should be equipped with a steering stabilizer that will prevent head shake during higher speeds and

A steering stabilizer is essential for preventing head shake on high speed straights. (Photo by Johnathan Edwards.)

over the bumps. It should be in good condition and checked over before each ride. This is important because in order to go fast on a motorcycle, the rider must have confidence in the machine. For example, if you feel the potential for a transmission problem, high speed straights may be dangerous. The suspension should also be set for the rider's height and weight, as proper suspension can keep a rider out of trouble. Finally, the tires should be in good condition, appropriate for the terrain selected and with adequate tire pressure.

Scanning is a technique riders can use to maximize safety during high speeds. The rider looks as far forward as possible and then back. Start referencing from the front wheel, forward and then back again; at 100 mph, objects are coming very fast. Always be prepared in case you hit something. This means maintaining an attack position,

keeping a firm grip on the bars and keeping your body in a forward centered position. A firm grip allows control of the bike, so in an instant you can correct the bike using your legs and upper body. Note, a firm grip does not mean to hold on as tight as possible; some looseness is needed to soak up the bumps.

Acceleration after entering a potential high speed straight should be done only after looking ahead for oncoming objects and knowing what type of terrain lies ahead. For example, look to see if there are rocks in the road. Most importantly check your road book or GPS before accelerating.

Looking at your road book and GPS while you ride can be dangerous. It is better to miss a turn rather than crashing because you were looking at the road book while traveling at a high rate of speed. Marc Coma says that it is a reflex for him to just slow down before looking at the road book or GPS. Knowing the road book can literally save your life.

High speeds in sand can be a bit tricky. The front wheel may want to move around or wobble; this is completely normal. To maintain speed in sand, keep a firm grip on the bars and move your weight back as far as possible.

Maintaining high speeds with rocks on the road is dangerous business. However, this is a skill that separates

KTM Red Bull Rally Team Tips for High Speed Straights

1. Scan the terrain, looking forward and then back—referencing from the front wheel

2. Keep a firm grip, to be prepared if you hit something

3. Use a steering stabilizer

4. Upper body strength is important

5. Maintain acceleration in order to bring the bike back in to straight motion

6. Body position should be neutral to leaning slightly forward

7. Remember, the goal of an adventure ride is to finish, going fast is second priority

many off-road racers. Some riders are better able to react more effectively at faster speeds than others, which is a talent in itself. Maintaining high speeds with rocks in the road becomes a balance between going fast and keeping a speed that is comfortable to the rider in case he hits a rock and needs to correct the motorcycle. Having a mousse insert instead of an inner tube can make a lot of difference. With a mousse, the rider can hit rocks straight on without worrying about a flat. Many mistakes are made when riders try to miss rocks or other objects at high speeds.

Trying to maintain high speeds in whoops is even more of a challenge. A long section of whoops exploits a rider's abilities rapidly. Upper body strength is essential, as well as standing up and leaning back in attack position. However, in a high speed whoop section scanning is harder because of the physical strain on the body along with the movement of the head.

Upper body strength is especially important when you hit an object with the motorcycle, because with good upper body strength, you can bring the bike back straight and center after hitting something. If you encounter head shake at high speeds, accelerate and sit back to straighten the bike; tapping the rear brake may help. When you hit something, hold the throttle open in order to bring the bike back into straight motion.

Finally, if you are tired and find your self comfortable—slow down. Many high speed falls occur for this very reason. Being comfortable or habituated is not a desirable thing when traveling at high speeds; you want the maximum alertness possible.

No matter if you are in the Dakar Rally or on an adventure ride, be prepared for animals. In general, burros and donkeys will not move out of the way; this is also true for camels and sometimes cows. Experience is the key to going fast on a motorcycle over any terrain. Always ask the experts how they do it, and stick to the basics.

Chapter 6

PHYSICAL CONDITIONING, INJURIES AND TRAINING

Just tell yourself, it is really never as bad as it seems ~ Scot Harden

Photo by G. Soldano

The physical aspect of riding a rally motorcycle is inescapable. Several examples have been discussed where good physical conditioning makes the difference between enjoying or suffering through an adventure ride. For example, picking up your rally bike in the sand dunes, stopping in the middle of a climb, holding on to the bike through a long section of camel grass, and the list continues. Most adventure riders have little time to train, but riding the bike and hitting the gym a few times a week can have a positive impact on your physical conditioning. Remember, what is important is how you make use of your time in the gym.

An excerpt from the KTM team medical journal illustrates the harsh conditions during the Dakar Rally:

I have been pushing the fluids on the riders and keeping up their nutrition, trying hard to keep the riders from drinking Cokes. Kellon and Chris still have no clue what is really ahead. The third stage in Morocco is cancelled due to fog, so we all meet in the fourth stage at the bivouac in Morocco. I can see that two thousand plus miles of road riding is starting to takes its toll on the riders, especially on their lower back muscles and hands.

Weight training

The Italian Fabrizio Meoni was considered to be the icon of rally racing. At 47 years old, he was among the fittest of riders. Much of his life revolved around his training schedule, which he followed with passion. His normal training routine consisted of three to four long distance cycling sessions. Meoni lived in a mountainous area of southern Italy called Castiglion Fiorentino and he trained climbing hills on a bicycle, which greatly helped his leg strength and stamina. His gym routine consisted of working his upper body about three times per week and legs two times per week. His workouts, like his personality, must have been intense.

Muscular strength is very important in the Dakar Rally. The idea that a person must be capable of riding twenty days straight, lifting a 400 plus pound rally bike and negotiating two hours of camel grass is exhausting just thinking about it. With the high speeds reached during a rally or adventure ride, control is paramount. Upper body and leg strength are important because we use the legs to turn the motorcycle, and

An example of circuit training that works the mid, upper, and lower body. 1. Abdominal crunches. 2. Bench presses. 3. One-legged squats. (Photos by Stephan Legrand.)

Cycling is an excellent tool for interval training. (Photo by Stephan Legrand.)

body. Remember to consume protein within 30 minutes of finishing your workout.

Interval training

Imagine picking up your bike in the sand dunes five times in succession in 100 degree temperatures, your heart rate soaring to nearly maximum and then having to recover. How can you prepare for this kind of effort? Interval training stresses the anaerobic energy system, otherwise known as the lactic

A rider picking up his bike in the Mauritanian sand dunes. (Photo by Jean Aignan Museau.)

important, but having so little time to spend training. However, going to the gym two or three times per week can be sufficient if done properly.

Circuit training is an efficient and effective means of building strength. If started some weeks in advance, circuit

abdomen, biceps, back and chest can be performed in thirty minutes. Choose the appropriate machines or weights, and move through each exercise completing a circuit. Usually, three to four circuits suffice. A similar routine can be done with the lower acid system. Interval training allows you to increase your heart rate and then recover; it is basically performing cardiovascular exercises reaching near maximum heart rate and then resting until the next interval. Most athletes use cycling or running to perform interval training.

During these intense efforts, many different reactions are occurring inside the body. One of these reactions is the production of lactic acid. When more lactic acid accumulates in the muscles (more is being produced than can be removed), you enter a state called lactic acidosis. By performing intervals that put the body into this state, several positive training adaptations occur. The most important training effect from these workouts is a higher power output at maximal effort, or VO2 max. For example, using a bicycle, warm up for five minutes. Then perform a near maximal effort for one minute and rest for four minutes. Repeat another one minute maximal effort interval and rest for three minutes. Perform another interval, rest for two minutes, and so on.

Massage

Massage is taken seriously in the Dakar Rally. Most teams in the rally have a personal massage therapist for the riders and even the mechanics. The riders put in thousands of miles, often without adequate rest.

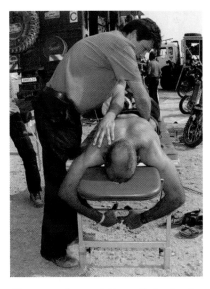

Massage is a daily activity in the bivouac during the Dakar rally. (Photo by J. Cunha.)

This causes a lot of wear and tear on the body and massage helps to bridge the gap to recovery. Usually about the fifth or sixth day of the rally, the riders complain of lower back and arm pains. The soreness then migrates to the mid and upper back, and finally to the neck, shoulders and hands. Near the end of the rally, most everything is sore on the body.

Massage helps for many reasons. Importantly, it provides a time for the rider to rest and forget about everything, helping in preparation for the next day. Massage improves blood flow in muscles which aides in recovery and reduces the chance for injury by improving flexibility and range of motion. The type of massage performed in the Dakar Rally is usually a deep tissue massage, which may be uncomfortable at first, and later soothing and relaxing. Most massage sessions take fifteen minutes to an hour to complete.

The KTM Red Bull team doctor performs easily over thirty hours of massage during the Dakar Rally on the American team.

Stretching for off-road riding

During an adventure ride, everyone is on the trail first thing in the morning. Inevitably, someone is late and riding fast trying to catch up. He falls, often sustaining a muscle or tendon injury. Injuries occur frequently when unprepared muscles and tendons are suddenly called into peak performance, such as riding a motorcycle without warming up.

As the body ages, injuring tendons and muscles is easier and more frequent. Muscle strains or pulls are the most common injures seen by sports medicine practitioners. Stretching is one of the most overlooked exercises in sports but certainly one of the most important. Stretching decreases chance of injury and keeps reflexes fast. As most of us are "coming of age," stretching becomes essential to continue a high level of off-road riding.

Muscles and tendons are less likely to be injured if their elastic characteristics are constantly trained through stretching. Poor training techniques, muscle and joint injury and immobilization after trauma lead to varying degrees of muscle and tendon injuries.

Certain injuries specific to riding occur secondary

to limitations in range of motion:

• Lower back pain / groin pulls: A lack of hamstring tendon flexibility.

• Carpal Tunnel syndrome: Results from repetitive movements, but also occurs from lack of flexibility in wrist and hand joints.

• Knee pain: A lack of both hamstring and quadriceps tendon flexibility.

Stretching properly is complex and should be performed much like an exercise. The idea is to stretch the soft tissue structures such as muscle, tendon, ligament and joint capsule. The connective tissue in and around the muscle contributes to most of the resistance to stretching; it is not the elastic muscle tissue itself.

Stretching vs. Warm Up

Warm up differs from stretching. Warm up activities should raise the temperature of the muscles and total body temperature in addition to increasing blood flow to these areas. A warm muscle contracts more forcefully and relaxes more quickly, thus improving speed and strength. A proper warm up will decrease injuries, and the heart is no exception to this rule.

The question often arises about how long to perform warm up exercises. A warm up exercise should be long enough

Stretching prior to riding is important to prevent injuries during the Dakar rally. (Photo by Johnathan Edwards.)

to increase body temperature but not cause fatigue; timing it closely to the start of the event will give the best results in terms of performance. The warm up should be tapered off about 10 to 15 minutes before an event. This will allow recovery from any slight fatigue without losing the effects of the warm up. Nowadays, in a competitive race, many riders warm up with stationary bicycles.

On an adventure ride, one would optimally start riding slowly to warm up and then get off the bike and perform a stretching routine. A more realistic method is to begin riding, then, after you are warmed up, stretch whenever you get off the bike. Your

stretching routine should include at least the following: shoulders, wrists, fingers, lower back, hamstrings, and quadriceps.

Proper Stretching

Many types of stretching exist, but here we will focus on passive static stretching. Static stretching involves placing muscles near their greatest length for 15-30 seconds. Static stretching is done by slowly moving the joint to the end of the range of motion to increase flexibility safely and effectively. One must avoid bouncing as this may cause tiny injuries called "microtears." Continue increasing the stretch position but *not* to the point of pain; a

Stretching should give a pulling feeling, not pain. (Photo by Johnathan Edwards.)

"pulling" feeling is acceptable. Safety is the main feature of passive static stretching. By keeping the muscles and tendons stretched, you can avoid injuries.

Flexibility varies from joint to joint. This is important because paying attention to how a muscle feels when properly stretched will reduce tissue

---

Improved flexibility can:

1. Increase efficiency and performance by requiring less energy to move a joint.

2. Decrease injury by augmenting tissue extensibility.

3. Improve neuromuscular coordination; that is, muscular balance and postural awareness.

4. Improve range of motion.

5. Improve blood circulation in and around the muscles.

6. Reduce post-exercise tightness and soreness.

---

tearing. If the feeling of a stretch increases in intensity as the position is being held, the person has most likely over stretched and should be advised to ease off. Regardless of the method used, the feeling of the stretch indicates when it is being done correctly.

In summary, the "stretched" feeling should be mild, comfortable, and not painful. Stretch to the point of a "pulling" sensation and hold for 15 to 30 seconds. Again, the "no pain, no gain" philosophy does not apply.

Proprioception and off-road riding

What does a word like proprioception have to do with off-road riding? Proprioception has to do with equilibrium or balance; more importantly it has the potential to decrease riding injuries, particularly in the knee, ankle and foot. Gymnasts are known to have superior proprioception; that is, they know precisely where their feet are in space no matter the orientation. They can land on small beams about the size of foot pegs. If you have ever broken or sprained your foot, ankle or knee, had anterior cruciate ligament reconstruction or arthroscopic knee surgery, proprioception exercises can help you tremendously. You can incorporate proprioception into your everyday workouts. In off-road riding terms, knowing where your feet are on the foot pegs

Proprioception exercises improve balance and prevent injuries. Notice that the eyes are closed. (Photo by Stephan Legrand.)

without looking at them is very important, even if you are in a berm or jumping through the air.

Proprioception can also be thought of your muscles, tendons, and joints working in synchrony to keep your balance. Try standing one legged, watch the muscles that are working in synchrony in your legs and feet to keep you from falling. In fact, the muscles work synchronously like an orchestra to maintain balance. By having superior proprioception, you can decrease chances of your feet coming off the pegs and improve your chances of putting your foot back on the peg.

Proprioception can be lost after knee and ankle injuries, which explains why off-road racers often re-injure themselves. Gymnasts constantly work on proprioception as they often injure their ankles and this helps decrease the chance of a repeat injury. If you have a previous ankle or knee injury, the proprioception exercises presented here may help you prevent re-injury.

One improves proprioception through practice. A basic way to practice proprioception is to balance on one foot with your arms to your sides. Try this for two to three minutes on each foot. Then do the same and close your eyes; you will probably fall over quickly. As you practice with your eyes closed, your muscles work intensely to keep you in balance. You will improve with each session and ideally perform these exercises at least once a day; if you have an injured ankle or knee, three times a day would be ideal. Gymnasts can remain on one foot with their eyes closed for well over five minutes without falling.

Another way to practice proprioception is on a tilt or wobble board like you may find in a gym or physical therapy office. Start off with a unidirectional board and then progress to a multi-directional board. Walking or running backward and sideways will improve proprioception.

In the weight room, one can do a type of leg exercise called the one legged squat. With a squatting bar or weights in each hand, step forward with one foot and perform a knee bend and come back again to a standing position. Repeat this about 15-25 repetitions on each leg.

Injury and treatment

Injury is an unfortunate reality when adventure riding or racing Dakar. We are often asked what our motivation is for riding motorcycles. After all, the sport is dangerous, injuries are frequent and some actually lose their lives. The best thing we can do to avoid injury is practice prevention. Riders must be able to know what is coming through the dust and make accurate judgments. They must know when to push or when to simply back off the throttle. Anyone can open the throttle and push forward, but to push for eighteen days without injury in Dakar is nearly impossible. Anyone who has participated in the Dakar Rally can attest to this. Knowing when to ride a section conservatively or push forward

Dakar Rally veteran Alfie Cox explains his shoulder injury during the 2005 Dakar rally. (Photo by Johnathan Edwards.)

is the real strategy to the Dakar Rally.

Here are more actual events from the 2005 rally, as recorded in the KTM Team medical journal:

The *fourth stage begins, and all I hear is that the Spanish*

High speed crashes can be very serious because of the weight of the motorcycle. (Photo by Jean Aignan Museau.)

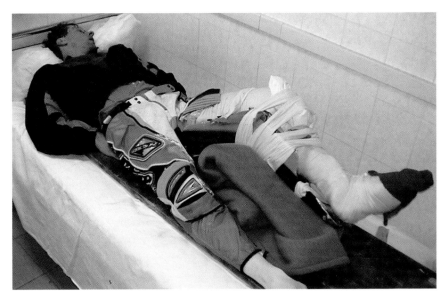

Using a motorcycle seat to immobilize the leg until medical help is reached. (Photo by Thomas McDonald.)

rider, Jordi Duran, has crashed very hard, breaking both femurs, his elbow, collar bone, wrist and ribs and suffering a concussion. Next, we hear that Kellon Walch crashed at the same place; he did not see the wash and crashed at nearly the same speed. His bike is damaged and his left shoulder is hurt, but he is able to get back up and finish out the stage. Chris Blais and Scot Harden finish the stage unscathed. The crash greatly affected Scot's morale. As Kellon pulls in, I can see he is protecting his shoulder; the shoulder is sore, but stable. With hydration, ice and anti-inflammatory medications, he is ready to ride again.

Injuries can occur at any time, without warning. Usually, an injury or fall is just a matter of time. Kellon's shoulder injury could have taken him out of the rally, but treating it right away

helped greatly. Jay Karsmaker, son of the famous motocross racer Pierres Karsmaker, presented with a shoulder injury more severe than Kellon's. He was treated with ice and taping to give his shoulder extra support, and anti-inflammatory medications for the pain. Like Kellon, Jay was able to finish the Dakar Rally, although afterwards he needed surgery to repair the damage to his shoulder. He fully recovered.

Another example of practical treatment of an injury occurred during stage 8 of the 2005 Dakar Rally when Scot Harden, who was riding through a section of sand at a high rate of speed when stuck his foot down and twisted his leg badly. The impact nearly ripped him off of his motorcycle and severely injured his left groin, leaving him unsure that he could continue.

The first and perhaps most important mode of medical

treatment for Scot's groin injury was reassurance. Nearly half way into the rally, Scot's mental outlook was noticeably weaker. A lack of sleep, witnessing Jordi Duran's crash as well as his own near-crash as he launched off a 30 foot sand dune all impacted his mental state. Although he was treated aggressively, Scot can tell you that even more important was what he told himself: "It is never as bad as seems."

The second mode of treatment for Scot's injury involved a basic tenant of sports medicine: Rest, Ice,

Many injuries in rally racing occur from fatigue and sleep deprivation. (Photo by Thorsten Flechsig.)

Compression, and Elevation (R.I.C.E.). Activated dry ice packs were placed on the groin, compression bandages were applied and his leg was kept elevated in extension. His discomfort was controlled with anti-inflammatory and pain

Treatment of Sports Injuries

R. **Rest** the injured limb.
I. **Ice** the injury.
C. Place a **compression** bandage on the affected limb.
E. **Elevate** the injured extremity.

medications, and he was urged to drink plenty of fluids. Prior to the start of the next stage, his leg and groin area were taped specific to treating a groin injury and then wrapped fairly tightly with a compression bandage.

Ice and anti-inflammatory medications can be real life savers on a rally. They generally do not affect thinking or alertness, and they help with general muscle soreness as well as with the bumps and bruises that come with riding hundreds of miles each day. After treating the injury with R.I.C.E., anti-inflammatory medications should be the first line treatment for an injury if medications are considered.

The third mode of treatment is to enable the rider to continue competing with tolerable pain; this helps prevent further injury. Scot was injected with pain medications that would not affect his thinking. He was given a sachet of pain-killers and was instructed to take them only if the pain became severe. These kinds of measures may enable an injured rider to finish the

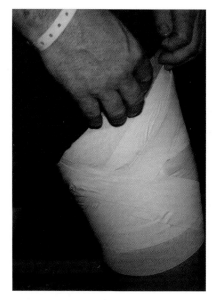

Groin injuries can be treated with taping and pain control. (Photo by Johnathan Edwards.)

stage and get him back the bivouac. It is not recommended to ride with narcotic pain medications, but there are times when they are beneficial and can be the difference between finishing or not. Scot rode through the next day, which was the infamous stage eleven of endless camel grass. At the finish of the stage he was very sore, but able to ride. The following day was a rest day. Scot wisely rested his leg the entire day, continuing to control the pain and the inflammation. With these treatments and Scot's persistence, he was able to the finish the Dakar Rally.

First aid on an adventure ride

Adventure and rally riding is an inherently dangerous sport and injuries are bound to occur.

If you should come upon a fallen rider, stop behind the rider blocking the trail so others may know to stop and help. Take off your helmet, jacket and gloves. Then observe the fallen rider and ask if he or she is all right. If you have a response, you know three essential things immediately: The rider (A) has an airway, (B) is breathing, and (C) has a pulse and adequate blood pressure. These are called the ABC's of emergency care.

Next, ask if he or she hurts anywhere and look for obvious injuries. A common question is whether or not to remove the helmet. A good rule of thumb is to always leave the helmet on

ABCs of Basic Life Support

A. **Airway**—Look, listen.
B. **Breathing**—Observe for respirations.
C. **Circulation**—Feel for a pulse and look at color of skin.

because it serves to keep the neck in a neutral position and removing a helmet incorrectly can lead to serious injury. However, if the rider says he or she has no pain and is able to take off the helmet without assistance, then it is usually not a problem to remove the helmet.

If the rider injures an ankle, leave the boot on as it acts like a splint and immobilizer until adequate medical assistance is received. If the leg hurts or is obviously broken, then immobilize it with straight pieces of wood or use the seat of the motorcycle to keep the leg straight and immobile.

If you come upon a serious situation, such as a rider who is not breathing or struggling to breath, it may be necessary to remove the helmet and gain access to the person's airway. A case in point occurred during a Baja Mexico race, when Honda rider Johnny Campbell crashed at high rate of speed and teammate Andy Grider came upon him first. Andy explained that he was at a loss for what to do. He observed Johnny breathing very irregularly and, in Andy's words, "not looking so good." In this case, when someone is having difficulty breathing, look in the mouth for obvious obstruction like dirt or rocks. If the breath does not sound clear, then gently lift the chin to try and relieve the obstruction. This is an extreme situation and medical assistance should be called for immediately.

Ideally, every rider should have participated in a First Aid course prior to entering a rally. The ability to maintain an airway, give mouth to mouth resuscitation or deal with a bleeding wound may be necessary. The critical issue is that of rapid assessment and intervention by a trained medical team. Your role is to summon help by satellite or cell phone, giving details and a GPS location.

Chapter 7

NUTRITION FOR ADVENTURE RIDING

Water sustains all.

Photo by Maindruphoto.

Riders ask frequently which nutrients are best before, during, and after a ride and if water alone is sufficient for fluid hydration. Often, people often receive conflicting and confusing information about nutrition, which is colored by marketing hype. An article is always written on the "next big breakthrough" in sports nutrition, and it usually conflicts with the previous month's article. Nutrition is a difficult subject for most riders because there is so much information to process and a personal nutritionist is a luxury few can afford.

Timing is everything

It does make a difference when nutrients are consumed. For example, there is strong evidence that when an exercise is finished, the glycogen (energy source for the muscles) inside of the muscle is depleted and must be refilled. Starting with before and during the ride, and then after the ride, we will illustrate what to consume as well as some of the reasons why.

Fueling muscles before and during exercise

For many riders, stretching comes before hitting the trails. However, proper nutrition should be the first exercise. Many times riders just drink a cup of coffee and then hit the trails; this is not enough. Since one never knows what an adventure ride will bring, it is prudent to assume that challenging physical difficulties will arise during the day.

Because of the dramatic effects of dehydration on sports performance, consuming 15 to 20 ounces of a sports drink with electrolytes about thirty minutes prior to prolonged exercise is beneficial; drink even more in extreme weather. Eating breakfast is also very important, but keep in mind to consume fluids and not just a cup of coffee. This pre-exercise drink delays dehydration, speeds the onset of sweating, keeps body temperature down and helps initiate glucose absorption during exercise.

During exercise, consuming sport drinks is important because it provides glucose to the muscles, decreases muscle damage and aids in recovery after the workout. More importantly, a glucose solution during a ride will prolong your mental and physical ability to perform on the trails.

A practical example of fueling muscles is an experiment where trained cyclists, all riding at the same difficulty level, are given either (1) nothing, (2) water, or (3) a glucose solution to drink during exercise. The cyclist without water lasts less than one hour and then his muscles call it caputs; the cyclist with water lasts between one and two hours; and the cyclist with a glucose solution lasts about two to four hours at the same intensity. This demonstration is important because it shows that muscles actually can use glucose during exercise; thus what you put in your hydration system (a.k.a camelback) is very important.

Muscle physiology

To better appreciate the timing of proper nutrients, it is important to understand how muscles use nutrients for energy during exercise, and the consequences of energy production.

During a ride, the first priority of a muscle is to generate large amounts of energy to keep the body in motion. The quality of muscles can be compared to the engine of a car. In order to work, muscles require a constant supply of energy to drive the wheels. Because internal combustion generates consider-able quantities of heat, the engine must be continuously cooled; otherwise the engine will lock up and stop.

During high intensity exercise, your muscles replenish energy by different mechanisms. On a simple level, one mechanism is with oxygen (aerobic) and the other is without oxygen (anaerobic). The aerobic pathway is used during riding, oxygen is being replaced and the energy mostly comes from glucose taken from the muscles. The anaerobic pathway is the one used when you are falling and picking up the rally bike in the sand multiple times and your heart rate is beating two hundred times per minute. If you overuse the anaerobic pathway, severe fatigue is guaranteed. The more you train, the more you can use the anaerobic pathway and recover from it.

Normally the body uses glucose or carbohydrates, but when your body is physically taxed, as on the tenth day of a hard Dakar Rally, the body may begin to use fats and protein, especially if you are stranded in the desert for a period of time; this also means the body is having a hard time utilizing glucose from the muscles. Considering all these factors, one can see the importance of eating the proper nutrients and at the correct times.

Sport drinks

The timing of drinking fluids during exercise depends on the intensity of the workout. Generally, 7 ounces of seven percent glucose solution every fifteen minutes will provide 27 ounces of fluid per hour. You can make up for lost fluids at a check point or if you stop on the trail. Assuming you lose two pounds of sweat during exercise, you need at minimum, thirty-two ounces of replacement fluid. As a general rule if you are sweating profusely, you should try to consume as much fluid as possible—preferably fluid with a glucose solution.

Sport drinks improve endurance and decrease fatigue. (Photo by Johnathan Edwards.)

Another dilemma of consuming sport drinks during exercise is choosing one that you like and does not cause stomach upset. When a sports drink is too sweet or concentrated, stomach upset results. Experiment with different sport drinks and flavors during exercise and formulate your own preference. Furthermore, unless you train yourself to drink during exercise, you will not do it during a rally or adventure ride. Athletes left to voluntarily drink during exercise will only replace about half of what they need. Finally, drinking a sports drink will stimulate you to drink more, unlike water which quenches the thirst.

Other nutrients such as adding protein to a sports drink may improve endurance even more and again aids in absorption of glucose. More importantly, the level of muscle damage may be decreased by adding protein to a sports drink; for those riding and training everyday, this can be very important. Many nutrition companies make a protein drink that mixes easily into solution.

After the ride

There are many causes of exercise related fatigue; most of them are a result of the muscles continually demanding energy. Fatigue is also often caused by the stress of heat and dehydration, which occurs in the deserts of the Dakar Rally.

The ability of muscles to regenerate energy decreases rapidly after a workout, so nutrients consumed after a certain "window of time" will have less of an impact in helping muscle recovery. This "window of opportunity" exists for about 30 to 60 minutes to replenish the muscle with glycogen. The "window phenomenon" applies both to glycogen and protein in the muscle, although to different degrees. The moral of the story is to consume something immediately after you ride, preferably a natural glucose source like a banana along with a sports drink to give your muscles energy needed for the next day.

More is not better

The body can only absorb so much glucose and the rest that is consumed goes to waste. Thus a specific amount of carbohydrates and proteins should be taken in after a hard workout. For example, after a long day on the trail, a piece of fruit, a sports bar and a bottle of water or sports drink is usually a good start.

A good regime to follow is one where thirty minutes before the exercise, you fully re-hydrate and raise blood glucose levels. During the exercise, continue hydrating with a sports drink; the goal here is to replace fluid and electrolytes, preserve muscle glycogen, and maintain blood glucose levels to set the stage for a faster recovery. Within thirty minutes after exercise, replenish muscle glycogen stores, initiate tissue repair and muscle growth, start the replenishment.

Dehydration

Dehydration is a given on any ride; assume it is going to happen and prepare properly. The consequences of dehydration are many, and understanding why it happens is important. What fluids should one drink to avoid dehydration? Human beings can only live five days without water in a moderate climate. The Dakar Rally with its harsh climate is no stranger to dehydration.

Always take the gas and drink fluids as 2005 Dakar champion Cyril Despres demonstrates. (Photo by G. Soldano.)

Life takes place in an aqueous medium. Human beings are made up mostly of water, in roughly the same percentage as water is to the surface of the earth. Because the physical and chemical properties of water are well suited to the requirements of life, it is no accident that life is a water-based phenomenon. Respiration, digestion, metabolism, waste removal, and temperature regulation are bodily functions that can only be performed with the presence of water.

Water is around most of the time, and it is often the solution to many adverse events. We dowse fire with water, clean wounds with water, flush dirt from the eye with water, quench thirst with water—and the list goes on and on. The adverse conditions of adventure riding demand water, as dehydration is a very serious medical condition. Even with the excellent organization of the Dakar Rally and most adventure rides, you must take matters in your own hands and drink and carry appropriate amounts of fluids.

The KTM Red Bull riders drink about 3-4 liters of sport drink per day, which contain glucose and electrolytes; this is very important, as the Dakar Rally is a race of nerves and the ability to race without sleep and continue long distances. If any one of the body's electrolytes are off, such as sodium for example, reflexes will decrease, the ability to think clearly decreases and mental fatigue sets in faster. It is critical to keep drinking fluids and taking in electrolytes, even when you feel you do not need them. Halfway through the rally, riding is often done on auto-pilot. The fatigue is incredible; it is akin to being in a torture chamber and being worked over to the point where the spirit and the mind just does not care anymore.

Muscles are very efficient at converting fuel into energy, but not perfect. Excess energy is converted into heat. In general, sixty percent of the heat generated is wasted; compared to seventy percent lost heat from a motorcycle engine. Like the radiator on an engine, it is important to remove excess heat to keep the body working at an optimum. If body temperature rises up to 102 degrees Fahrenheit (39° celsius), exercise performance is compromised, even in cold conditions. The body is very good at dispersing heat by sweat evaporation, although we inhibit this somewhat by the gear we ride with. As the heart works harder to move the blood circulation around in order to sweat properly, lactic acid forms and fatigue ensues. To put it into perspective, even a two percent dehydration level affects athletic performance. Mental and physical abilities decrease as well as stamina and fine motor and coordination skills. You can sense when you are three percent dehydrated because you are thirsty; at four percent dehydration heat cramps ensue along with dizziness and nausea.

How do you know when to drink fluids? If you are starting a ride thirsty, you are already dehydrated. Thus, it is important to start drinking days before a planned ride or adventure tour.

KTM Red Bull factory rider Andy Grider drinks about 3-4 liters of sport drink per day during the Dakar rally. (Photo by Johnathan Edwards.)

The amount one should drink depends on the fitness level of the rider and the difficulty of the ride, including terrain and temperature.

What do you drink in your hydration system?

Many people say you should only drink water. We suggest that adding glucose and electrolytes to your hydration packs improves riding as well as safety. Water alone will not sufficiently replace electrolytes. In fact, drinking too much water can decrease the amount of sodium in the body and lead to mental fatigue. An interesting study involving cyclists showed that one could nearly double the time before the muscles become fatigued by using a 6-8% glucose drink compared to those cyclists drinking only water. This applies directly to off-road riding, as many of the rides last hours, sometimes days.

The brain uses sixty percent of the body's available glucose for proper function. If glucose levels are low or glycogen stores are inadequate, mistakes could be made which lead to (avoidable) crashes and injury. Remember to drink every 15 to 30 minutes, whether you are thirsty or not. This is called grazing, a concept often used in bicycle racing.

What type of sport drink should you use during rides? One that tastes good! If you put

Fill your hydration system with something you enjoy drinking. (Photo by Jean Aignan Museau.)

something in your hydration system that you do not like, you will have a lot of sport drink left over at the end of a ride. If you like the taste, you will keep drinking—this is a proven fact. The KTM Red Bull Dakar Rally team uses Champion Nutrition for sport drinks and protein replacement. Champion Nutrition products suit the team well because all of their products are pharmaceutical grade quality and taste good. Many products available today contain a lot of filler; filler is product to increase the bulk of the powder and does not contain the important proteins or electrolytes. Professional rally racer Andy Grider has stated several times that by using sport drinks before and during the races, he has seen an increase

in his endurance. His 3rd place finish in the Tunisia rally, 2nd place finish in 2004 Baja 1000 and his win in the San Felipe 250 support his statements.

Electrolytes and thinking

Sodium, potassium, and calcium are among the important electrolytes which exist in the body. Even a small drop in sodium can cause mental changes, including dizziness, decreased reaction times and mental alertness—all of which are paramount in any ride. Potassium is important in many processes in the body, but the one that most people relate to is muscle soreness and cramps. A low potassium level will contribute to muscle spasms that make riding uncomfortable, and sometimes impossible. Bananas and other fruits contain potassium. Replacing electrolytes can be done via fluids as well as protein. Many sport drinks contain appropriate amounts of electrolytes and should be used in addition to regular meals.

A consequence of sweating is losing electrolytes, including sodium, potassium and chloride, all of which are necessary for metabolic functions, muscle contractions and nerve transmission. Muscular fatigue and cramps are usually a result of potassium loss. Hyponatremia occurs when water and sodium are lost in the sweat and not replaced.

The ideal composition for a sports drink may be the following: glucose 20 - 26 grams, whey protein 5 - 6 grams, sodium 100 - 250 mg, potassium 60 - 100 mg. (Photo by Johnathan Edwards.)

Symptoms include fatigue, decreased mental alertness, dizziness, cramping, nausea and even seizures. Acute hyponatremia is a medical emergency and athletes have died as a result. Hyponatremia is infrequent but must be taken seriously; prevention is the key to avoiding this syndrome.

Other consequences of exercise

Every time you take your car for a drive, there are residual effects. The fuel decreases, carbon builds up on the piston and wear on the engine parts occurs. The same applies to our bodies.

Muscle damage is an unavoidable consequence of riding long distances as witnessed during the Dakar Rally; however, some muscle damage is good since it stimulates the muscle rebuilding process. Muscle injury triggers acute inflammatory processes causing tissue and cell membrane damage. The inflammatory process may not peak for some hours. This is one of the reasons muscle soreness is not felt until after exercise is completed. The former is evident after a long and hard workout; the muscles ache and you do not have the same strength as before the exercise. Muscle damage is usually from a build up of lactic acid and overheating. This is where some of the specialty sports drinks come into play.

If you are working out hard enough, replacing glucose, protein, electrolytes and special antioxidants may help; this is especially true in the Dakar Rally. Energy is needed to repair the cell membranes; thus, you can imagine what dehydration and low glucose stores can do to a body.

Suppression of the immune system

Athletes who train hard and suffer from sleep deprivation are more susceptible to colds and infections. Also, when people travel in foreign countries and eat unusual foods, they are more susceptible to infection. There are several reasons for the immunosuppressive effects of strenuous exercise. One reason is that cortisol, a hormone associated with stress, increases with sleep deprivation and strenuous exercise. Additionally, glutamine, an amino acid, has been shown to be involved in the regulation of the immune system. Because glutamine levels decrease during strenuous exercise, consuming glutamine may help offset immunosuppressive effects. Above all, a good balanced diet is important.

Protein supplements

The final common denominator in any athletic event is what your muscles can do for you. Issues affecting off-road riders are strength and endurance. Think of the strength needed to lift a rally bike and then continue to the finish.

Building muscles is similar to building a house: many types of wood in various shapes and sizes are used to build a sturdy home. Likewise, many types of amino acids are used as the building blocks for protein, which is used to build your muscles. Imagine how the structure or strength of a house would be compromised if a critical piece of wood is missing. The same is true if one type of amino acid missing: protein and thus muscle may not be as strong when you try to use it.

Ten essential amino acids must be put into your body by food sources because your body cannot make them. To make protein effectively, it is

SOURCE	PROTEIN	CARBOHYDRATES	FAT
	(grams)	(grams)	(grams)
Eggs (whole)	6	0.6	5.5
Egg white	3	0.4	0.0
Egg yolk	3	0.0	5.5
3 oz.Chicken (skinless)	20.4	0.0	1.45
Avocado	4.0	4.8	30.8
Black Beans (1 cup)	44.6	122	3.0
Soy bean (1 cup)	19.8	19.4	10.3
3 oz. Tofu	7.8	2.4	4.2
Plain yogurt (1 cup)	12	16	3.5
Apple	0.27	21	0.5
Banana	1.2	27	0.5
4 oz Beef	20	0	23
Bagel	11	56	2.5
1 oz. Cheese(cheddar)	7	0.4	9.4
Milk (2%)	6	25.2	2.4

Protein supplements and bars should taste good, give you energy and improve your riding. (Photo by Stephan Legrand.)

incorrectly. More interestingly, one's psychological condition matters; people with a calm and healthy mind will make better proteins than an angry person.

The sources of protein are very important. One needs quality wood for a house just as one needs quality protein for the body. Quality protein contains large amounts of essential amino acids and does not contain a large amount of fat and carbohydrates. Egg protein has all of the essential amino acids and therefore is a high quality protein. In fact, it is a reference protein to which other proteins are compared.

Some examples of quality proteins are skinless chicken, turkey, most fish, beans, yogurt, oatmeal and, of course, protein supplements. Beef, pork and lamb all contain high quality proteins, but they are loaded with fat and cholesterol. Excessive consumption of red

very important to have the right amino acids and in the right amounts. To continue with our example, when building a house, we know it should not be raining. Ideally, the weather should be warm and, of course, we need a healthy crew.

Likewise, timing is also critical in building healthy muscle. The body must be healthy and warm. When you are sick, your body is concentrating on fighting bacteria and viruses, and will not give you any slack if you are eating meats has been linked to heart disease and some types of cancers.

Most serious athletes use some type of protein supplement. By increasing your metabolic rate by exercise, your protein requirement increases. Many top motorcycle racers like Marc Coma, Cyril Despres, Andy Grider, Chris Blais, Ty Davis and Jeremy McGrath use protein supplements. Some cyclists consume over 300 grams of protein per day.

When your body is pushed to the limits of muscle fatigue, it demands protein and carbohydrates. Your body must have the right amino acids and in the correct amounts, otherwise you will be making mainly fat and not muscle!

When should you take a protein supplement? Think of using protein supplements as a strategic move, since it is not something you take just when you are hungry. Most athletes begin protein loading in the morning and will make a protein shake or add a scoop of protein powder to their cereal or oatmeal. About an hour before your workout or after the workout, drink another protein shake, preferably with another high quality protein food source. Lastly, a protein drink with dinner or before bed should complete your protein for the day. The amount of protein you take in each day depends on how serious you are with training.

How fast will you see improvements in your muscles after you start taking protein supplements along with a daily training regimen? If you are starting to take protein supplements for the first time, or restarting after a long period of time, you may not see improvement in muscle bulk or strength right away. Medical literature shows it will be two weeks to a month before you see changes; increased strength comes first and then an increase in muscle size (assuming a daily training regimen).

By increasing muscle mass, you increase your metabolic rate. In fact, 60 to 75% of energy expended daily is from the muscles. Since muscle weighs nearly two times more than fat; you may see your weight increase even though you are becoming leaner. Lastly, remember that a protein supplement does not have any significant effect if you are not training, except for building more fat.

A protein supplement is a synthesized form of protein, and it is important to understand that not all protein supplements are equal. If you are working out, you need more protein than the daily-recommended amount (which is about 50 - 80 grams of protein per day, depending on which source you read). To increase your protein intake, you either have to eat a lot of food rich in protein or you could take supplements. Natural

sources of protein such as meat have the advantage of providing all of the proper amino acids and important vitamins and minerals. A good balance is to eat a natural source of protein and to use protein supplements.

Proteins modeled after natural sources (see table on page 57) are best. When a protein supplement is not as well refined, it means it may contain a lot of crude non-protein products known as filler. (It is cheaper for a company not to refine its products and to add filler to protein supplements.) Protein supplements are rated by World Health Organization (WHO), which verifies the quality of a protein. Proteins from whey and egg sources are usually very complete because they contain all of the essential amino acids in the correct amounts. Look for a protein supplement which is highly refined. Even though it may cost more, the product is better for you. If you are lactose intolerant, there are some lactose-free protein supplements.

Another concern of protein supplements is the taste. Most people will not drink something everyday if it tastes horrible. Most protein supplements come in a variety of flavors that you mix with milk or water; this constitutes a shake that is made in a blender. Other ways to improve the taste of a protein shake is to add fresh fruit (just cut it up). Yogurt or ice cream will make just about any protein shake taste good.

The next time you buy a protein supplement, consider factors like cost, taste, source, amino acid profile, how well refined the product is, and whether the supplement has vitamins and minerals.

Vitamins and performance

Many people take vitamins for better health, but there are ways to take vitamins strategically which can help in adventure riding. Vitamins B and C are very important and will be discussed here.

The B-vitamins are essential in providing the body with energy. Glucose is the usable energy and glycogen is the storage energy; the brain alone is dependent on sixty percent of the body's glucose supply. B-vitamins play a role in the conversion of glycogen to glucose; they also play key roles in the metabolism of fat and protein. Low levels of some B-vitamins can actually cause decreases in thinking ability, which can be a big problem in riding a rally bike.

B-vitamins are essential to how our reflexes work and muscles contract. They also affect reaction times and memory. Our reflexes are truly given to us so that we can hunt, avoid falling off cliffs and run from tigers. B-vitamins are essential to the nerves and muscles which allow us to pull in the clutch lever, turn the bars and instinctively avoid that boulder that is coming at us when we are traveling over 90 mph on a trail.

How do we know if we are taking in the correct amount of B-vitamins? By looking at our diet. All of the B-vitamins are found in brewer's yeast, liver, and whole grain cereals. Other sources include bran, wheat germ, eggs and many colorful veggies and fruits.

Low levels of vitamin B-1 (thiamine) may cause you to form more lactic acid than you want, leading to more muscle soreness. A deficiency in vitamin B-2 (riboflavin) impairs wound healing. Niacin is vitamin B-3. Niacin is used to treat high cholesterol and diarrhea, and a deficiency of niacin in the diet impairs one's ability to think. Low levels of vitamins B-6 and B-12 result in decreased energy. When glucose levels drop below normal, attention span is decreased and irritability is increased. Folic acid is an important B-vitamin which is closely linked to the health of your red blood cells as well as your memory. Finally, vitamin B-12 is important also for red blood cells, the brain and nerves. During the Dakar Rally, each rider, and even the mechanics receive a vitamin B-12 injection.

Energy drinks are very popular in sporting events and the KTM team is sponsored by Red Bull. The ingredients in most energy drinks include primary glucose, B-vitamins, caffeine and other elements. The B-vitamins and caffeine help alertness and allow the body to metabolize sugar more rapidly. The KTM Red Bull team uses Red Bull energy drinks to help with alertness during races. It is important to consume an energy drink only when you really need it. Otherwise you become habituated to the drink and it will lose its effectiveness. Riders often use energy drinks after a hard special test or while they are reviewing their road books for the next day. The importance of being alert while reading the road book cannot be stressed enough; as the road book can literally save your life.

The B-vitamin complex should be taken together. B-vitamins are important to many of the activities we enjoy in life and may even help us to perform at higher levels. Eating a well balanced diet will give us those vitamins and help us to maintain the memory, reflexes and muscle strength to survive the unnatural test we put our bodies through each day—such as the Dakar Rally.

Vitamin C

Vitamin C is also known as ascorbic acid and helps to maintain skin, bones, muscles and ligaments. It aids in wound healing and forming red blood cells, and is necessary for the function of the B vitamins.

During stress, the body rapidly uses up the stores of vitamin C. Cold weather, for example, increases the body's need for vitamin C.

Vitamin C is better absorbed via natural foods, such as fruits and vegetables, rather than pills. For example, if one takes two grams of vitamin C, only 50% is used by the body. If you are training seriously for Dakar, you should be supplementing vitamin C intake. Think of it as a "stress vitamin"—the more you stress the body, the more vitamin C you will need.

Summary

During prolonged off-road motorcycle riding, there are a number of metabolic, physiologic and hormonal changes that must occur if the energy needs of the muscles are to be met. As the muscles work, temporary adverse effects occur such as a loss of body water, depletion of glucose stores, muscle damage and suppression of the immune system. These adverse effects persist for long periods of time and are related to the duration and intensity of exercise. If these adverse effects are not addressed, recovery is stunted and athletic performance, physical and mental, is depressed. Appropriate nutrient supplementation results in greater endurance and recovery.

Chapter 8

RALLY AND ADVENTURE RIDING FOR THE 30+ YEAR OLD

The problem with the youth of today is that one is no longer part of it ~ Salvador Dali

Photo by G. Soldano.

You have finally arrived; this is your reward, pursuing adventure riding on your own terms. It is a rite of passage that you have achieved, and now you are focused on rally and adventure riding. Imagine that you just came back from a long off-road adventure trip. It is Monday morning and you have to go to work, but your back is killing you. What to do? A discussion of the pro's and con's of riding off-road riding beyond age 30 will help.

Learning better how to manage your body after riding as well as about the aging process, stretching, and nutrition are things a thirty plus year old athlete should begin to think about. Also, read some testimonials from some of the greats in our sport who managed to continue riding well past their prime.

When discussing rally and adventure riding for the over-30 year old, let's face it, Dali's quote applies here; we are no longer part of the youth.

Actually, the best rally racers in the world are in their 30's and 40's because they have a great combination of strength and stamina, in addition to mental

At 49 years old, Scot Harden is still riding each week, teaching adventure riding schools and competing at a professional level. (Photo by Thomas McDonald.)

At 47 years old, Fabrizio Meoni was one of the fittest rally athletes ever. His passion and fitness level allowed him to ride a motorcycle like no other. (Photo by Jean Aignan Museau.)

toughness and problem solving capabilities under pressure. They are much stronger in these areas than younger riders. Even in their early 50's these riders can take very good care of themselves.

A prime example is champion rally rider Scot Harden. He is almost 50 years old and still competitive in the Baja 1000 and Dakar Rally. In Scot's own words, "I don't see myself stopping any time soon, as I am in better shape than I was three years ago and will continue to maintain my fitness as a motivation to continue competing." Older riders should realize they have many things going for them and must work to maximize those assets.

The quote "old age and treachery shall overcome youth and skill" is very true. Therein lies the secrets of winning the

Dakar Rally. A beneficial factor for older athletes is that they are in a period in their life where they have figured out what they

are going to do. They have careers, education and family structure. They are focused. The whims and passing fancies of youth have been explored and older riders know what they really want.

Looking for authentic life experiences, older off-road riders seek something to take them out of their normal realm— not an easy task for most. For many riders, adventure riding is a pause from family life and career pressures, a great escape. However, with age comes responsibility. We are not all in a position where we can afford to hurt ourselves and we must approach our sport carefully. This is one reason why, after age 30, many riders switch from motocross to rally or adventure riding.

Temperatures may reach over 120 degrees Fahrenheit (45 degrees Celsius) in the African Sahara desert. (Photo by G. Soldano.)

Some of the negatives to being thirty-plus is that the body does not work as it did during youth. We cannot push ourselves relentlessly and unmercifully without taking care of ourselves along the way. We cannot just run wide open like a 20 year old rider can. We have to plan ahead and take certain precautions; this is where hydration, riding technique, and planning ahead all come into play. Hopefully, you have developed good fundamental riding skills. If not, you may have some really bad habits and some retraining has to take place.

The old analogy, "you cannot teach an old dog a new trick," is only true if the "old dog" is never shown what the new trick is. You can learn at any age. This is where we need to reevaluate what the new program is. If you constantly repeat the same mistakes, you will not get any better. This is where riding schools or adventure camps can help a lot.

Changes in the body after age 30

How does your body change with age? First, realize it is a natural process, but that there are things you can do to help. Your joints (knee, wrist, neck and back) stiffen with age due to cellular changes in the proteins (collagen) of ligaments and tendons and bone. Muscles change with age, although not as much as joints, tendons, and

Stretching often will help to prevent injuries. (Photo by Johnathan Edwards.)

ligaments. Muscles seem to maintain their full potential until you reach about 60 years of age. The bottom line is your muscles are capable of maintaining the same strength and flexibility as long as you remain active and use them. Exercising and remaining active help keep reflex times of muscle normal as well as maintaining flexibility of ligaments and tendons.

Bones maintain very good strength until about age thirty and decrease slowly in strength afterwards. Realize bone is constantly being remodeled— being broken down and re-made every moment of your life. Bone loss occurs in both men and women, but more so in women. What can you do to improve bone strength?

Jump up and down on your feet! It is true—remaining active with activities like jogging, riding off-road or weight lifting will keep your bones stronger longer. A weight stimulus tells the bone to keep on remodeling itself more efficiently and to maintain strength.

Not all bone strength decreases in the same manner. For example, the bones in your lower back lose density and strength faster than other bones; lower back pain is a result of this process. In fact, immobility causes your bones to weaken faster than anything; sitting on your buttocks causes the calcium to be ripped straight from the bones and this slows down bone remodeling big time. Immobilization causes muscles to atrophy at an alarming rate.

Ligaments and tendons become less elastic with age. As you get older, you are more likely to have sprains and strains in your ligaments and tendons; decreased range of motion in your shoulder, wrists and other joints may result. The former is especially true if you do not warm up or stretch properly. Remember, good nutrition also helps to keep the ligaments and tendons more elastic.

Stretching deserves a lot of mention here. If nothing else, please read about stretching! The key to decreasing injuries is to maintain flexibility. Injuries frequently occur when unprepared muscles and tendons are suddenly called into peak performance, such as in off-road riding. Stretching seems to be on everyone's "to do" list, but it is often the last to be done.

Suzuki team manager Roger Decoster is very active and still enjoys riding. He says he's used stretching throughout his motocross career and especially after injuries to speed up recovery time. What does stretching do for you? Stretching maximizes your range of motion and decreases injuries by keeping the ligaments, tendons and muscles flexible. Stretching improves blood flow to the tissues, tells the bones to maintain strength and increases neuromuscular coordination.

A common injury in off-road riding is pulling the groin

ligaments and tendons. In fact, a groin injury nearly took Scot Harden out of the 2005 Dakar Rally, but with daily treatment, he continued to the finish. By stretching and maintaining flexibility in the groin area, one can decrease the chance of a groin injury.

Shoulder and wrist injuries are also common in motorcycle racing. Typically, this occurs when riders try to catch themselves when falling in a turn. Stretching the shoulder and wrists can help decrease the severity of sprain and strain injuries to these areas.

How should you stretch? Stretching should not be a painful process nor should it be a burden. Stretching is best done after a brief warm-up period of exercise. The stretching technique should be slow and gradual, nothing like the torture your high school physical education teacher put you through. The "no pain, no gain" principle does not apply with stretching. The idea is to work at it slowly, and your body will adapt if you give it time. Avoid bouncing or stretching quickly. A stretch should not be painful; instead, it should be a mild, comfortable pull.

If you cannot touch your toes now, don't worry. Give it time and you will, without pain. Each stretch should last for about 30 seconds. Repeat a stretch 5-10 times. Symmetry is important; if you stretch one side, stretch the other. Consult your sports medicine physician

or other qualified personnel if you have questions.

Stretch your neck, shoulders, back, legs, ankles and groin before each ride. This sounds like a lot, but you should be able to come up with a stretching routine that lasts about 5-10 minutes. You should be able to perform stretches with your gear on (except the helmet). A great source for stretching is Bob Anderson's book, *Stretching*, available from Shelter publications. You can find it in local athletic and book stores.

Running

Running is any athlete's best friend when used properly, and a hard enemy to beat when not. Whether it is jogging, basketball or chasing the dog,

Running keeps you in shape and improves your riding endurance. (Photo by Stephan Legrand.)

running helps an athlete adapt to many situations. Running increases aerobic capacity (the ability to breath under stressful situations), increases bone strength, and helps with the heart and its pumping action.

One of the most important things the older athlete needs to know about running is how to prevent running-related injuries. First, keep it fun and don't overdo it. Overuse injuries are the most common for runners and are preventable by using the correct shoes and running on a consistent surface. Invest in quality shoes, as the support of running shoes breaks down after 3 to 6 months. Prevention is the key to avoiding running injuries. If your knees hurt, check the shoes and replace them. Shoe orthotics may prevent foot injuries. Soft shoe orthotics such as Sorbthane™ are available from athletic stores.

Nutrition

Nutrition for the 30-plus year old athlete is critical for many reasons. As one gets older, one usually consumes fewer calories as appetite decreases with age. Metabolism decreases about 2% per year up to a certain age. Good nutrition is important as the immune system weakens with age.

Nutrition is also important for recovery after a strenuous event. If you are going to take part in a challenging adventure

Ten time Baja 1000 winner, Larry Roseler completed his first Dakar rally at age 46. (Photo by Thomas McDonald.)

ride, nutritionally prep your body the same as you would prep your bike. Motocross champion Johnny O'Mara is over forty, and he is still one of the fittest motorcycle athletes ever. He continues to race mountain bikes at a professional level, runs everyday and still hammers a motocross bike through two tanks of gas once in a while. Johnny has noticed that as he gets older, he eats less than when he was younger and he is stricter about what he allows in his diet. He uses nutrition products to help him recover from exercise more efficiently.

Off-road riders often do not drink enough fluids. Why should you care? Because all the heavy gear off-road riders wear makes them especially sus-

ceptible to heat exhaustion— just refer to the Italian rider story in Chapter 11 for an example. Inadequate fluid intake causes your heart and brain to work harder, depriving valuable energy. Dehydration and lack of riding time are usually the reasons for arm pump, muscle cramps and fatigue on the race track. Calories from carbohydrates and protein are important for recovery and energy. Use sport drinks and eat sport bars for good sources of carbohydrates, and protein prior to and during each ride.

One last issue is calcium. Calcium is a major component of the bones and muscles. If you can tolerate milk, be sure to drink the recommended amount everyday. Calcium levels in the older person slightly decrease, making it an even more important issue. Great sources of calcium are orange juice fortified with calcium, milk, broccoli, and yogurt. Most authorities say 800-1000 mg per day is adequate. So "do your body good" with a proper diet combined with exercise and having fun.

Adventure riding / Rallies

How about adventure riding and rally racing in general? Should an older rider think about riding technique, equipment, and racing any differently than they did before age 30? Definitely yes! Dress for the crash, not the race; preparing for the fall is the key to preventing injuries. Everybody has to work on Monday, so take the extra effort to prevent injuries with effective riding gear, along with your stretching program.

Maintaining hydration is critical while riding in the higher temperatures of the Sahara desert. (Photo by DPPI.)

Elbow pads may seem uncomfortable at first, but think about a basic fall in a turn. The elbow always takes some kind of abuse and is usually not protected. Also, elbow pads keep your skin free of battle wounds that you may not want to show at work.

Now, about knee pads: how good are yours? Will they break just by dropping them, or will they actually take some abuse? Invest in a sturdy set of knee protectors.

Kidney belts—do they really protect the kidneys? Yes, and more. Kidney belts also protect the ribs and other internal organs from moving as much as they would otherwise. If your kidney belt is too small, get the right size and you will be thankful in years to come.

Larry Roseler and Paul Krause during the 2004 Dakar Rally. Both are very accomplished off-road riders and still race competitively today. (Photo by Thorsten Flechsig.)

Rarely does one hear of motorcycle riders wearing jock straps. Athletes wear them in wrestling and football—why not in off-road riding? For about five bucks, a comfortable and flexible strap will protect your genital organs and can prevent groin injuries.

What should you do in the event of an injury? Number one is to evaluate and treat as soon as possible. This becomes even more important in an older person. The faster you respond with treatment, the sooner you can be riding again and functioning normally.

For example, if you twist an ankle, the minimum you should do for this injury is to rest it, ice it, use a compressive dressing (ACE wrap) and elevate it. Remember the mnemonic R.I.C.E. If you are injured, use R.I.C.E. two to three times per day. Perform R.I.C.E. before and after rides, during your lunch break and at home. Be aggressive with the treatment. Do not simply wait for it to heal on its own.

Consult your physician if your injury persists, because it needs a professional evaluation. Be certain the physician treating you is one who understands sports and is experienced in sports injuries. This will usually be an orthopedic, family practice or a rehabilitation doctor.

Racing tips

Race with your head and use your legs to guide the

Giovanni Sala, at 42 years old, is one of the most accomplished rally and enduro riders ever. (Photo by DPPI.)

motorcycle. Scot Harden's philosophy is to think. He says, "think about what is going on around you and think about what you are doing out on the trails." Ask yourself, are you pre-occupied with something else besides riding? Practice racing smoothly and with finesse. Riding more efficiently should come with age, and you will save energy and go faster in the long run. Keep those elbows up and do not fight the bike; think smooth! And remember that you are having fun riding, as you explore nature and the outdoors. You are doing something that 75% of your co-workers do not do today in America, and that is staying in shape!

How about a situation where the older rider is a bit overweight? This is not an uncommon situation. A small investment in the suspension will make a world of difference on the track and allow you to have a lot more fun. KTM Red Bull mechanic Bret Leef observes that most heavy riders have their suspension too soft. He believes that using stiffer springs in both front and rear is one of the most important changes this type of rider can make.

Usually a much stiffer spring is needed; for example, 5.0 to a 5.6. Bret also suggests revalving the rebound dampening (how fast the shock moves up) on the rear shock to match the stiffer spring. The bottom line is to be sure your bike is set up properly—handlebars, seat height, suspension, and gearing.

So, is over thirty really over the hill? That depends on your philosophy and how much you train. A trained 45 year old is vastly different than an untrained 45 year old. Scot Harden will tell you, "You are as old as you feel, you just need a good attitude!"

Riders like Scot Harden, Larry Roseler, Mike Larocco and the late Fabrizio Meoni are living proof that a thirty-plus year old can compete at the highest level. Now that you have some fresh, new ideas in your cranium, hopefully you will act on your thoughts and become a more efficient and safer rider for yourself and those you ride with.

Chapter 9
PREPARING FOR THE RIDE OF YOUR LIFE

Photo by Stephan Legrand.

Life is on the wire...everything else is waiting ~ Karl Wellenda

Adventure riding is living in the legend, riding a motorcycle to venture out and explore new lands, dreams and who you really are. Preparation, knowing the bike and where you are going are most important, and then the rest falls into place. From the garage to the trails, preparing the bike for the type of terrain you are going to ride is important. Good tires, spare parts and tools can save the day. Food, coffee, medical supplies and maps are other essential items you will need to pack for the trip.

Planning a Ride

The first consideration is destination and distance. Review as much literature as possible about the places where you are going. Choose a start and finish point for the area of interest, and remember that these may change during the course of the trip.

Next, start checking maps and websites, such as www.adventurerider.com (see Appendix) to search the areas where you are going. Be sure to pay attention to dirt roads, BLM areas, little towns, forest areas, rivers, lakes, and anything else that could be used for course markers.

One problem with maps is that most do not show all the off-road routes available, as much of adventure riding is done via dirt roads and trails. For example, detailed maps for Baja Mexico exist, but the Mexican government distributes them, so it may take a little work obtaining one. Sometimes there are no maps at all, so inquire locally or ask someone who has ridden there in the past about their experiences.

GPS maps will also show some dirt roads and contacting the forestry service may be of benefit. Always save maps and information as well as accounts of what happened on past adventure rides. This information may be valuable in the future and it will help you prepare better for the next ride. Making a few notes in a journal can help greatly.

Weather Conditions

Surprises happen with even the most familiar terrain. Always check the weather patterns before going to ride. Spring showers will change riding conditions, even if you are familiar with the area. This is true for both on and off road. Expect road changes especially on steep mountain roads because of landslides or ice

Ten Rules to Live by While on an Adventure Ride

1. Take into account that great love and great achievements involve great risk.

2. When you lose, don't lose the lesson.

3. Follow the three R's: Respect for self, respect for others and responsibility for all your actions.

4. Don't let a little dispute injure a great friendship.

5. When you realize you've made a mistake, take immediate steps to correct it.

6. Spend some time alone every day.

7. Share your knowledge. It's a way to achieve immortality.

8. Be gentle with the earth.

9. Once a year, go some place you've never been before.

10. Judge your success by what you had to give up in order to get it.

Adventure riding means exploring new lands. *(Photo by Stephan Legrand.)*

best lines. Trails and quality of terrain change each day.

Preparing the motorcycle

As discussed in Chapter 2, adventure bikes are prepped similar to rally bikes, but with a different goal in mind; you are not trying to win a race and there are generally no mechanics, so everyone has to be completely self contained and capable of maintaining their bike.

After checking that everything is in proper working order, inspect the sprockets and chains. Many rookie bike

Joe Barker has ridden extensively through the French Alps on his KTM 950 Adventure bike. He completed 65 of the 76 passes which exist in France. Some of these passes include the famous L'alpe D'huez. *(Photo by Joe Barker.)*

and snow. When it rains, diesel spills from passing trucks make the road more slippery than expected. A lesson from off-road adventure riding is to never expect the trails to be the same over and over again. You really have no idea what is on the other side of the hill of curve ahead. The more off-road riding you do, the more attention is required to the trails. Ask yourself if you are choosing the problems come from chains and sprockets. Also, new tires and brake pads should be considered. You will not find these parts in the middle of nowhere!

Fuel

Knowing the fuel range of your motorcycle relative to the terrain and country you are travelling through is imperative. Remember that riding through sand consumes more gas than hard pack trails, and technical trails more than open flats. Gearing is important because it also affects fuel range. A motorcycle with a lower gear ratio is more fuel efficient.

On long adventure rides, Scot Harden advises having at least one rider on a motorcycle with a longer fuel range than the others because that motorcycle can go for help if needed. The smaller displacement engines are more fuel efficient than larger motorcycles.

Always take gas with you. Taking a chance on fuel stops is ill advised and will ruin any adventure ride. Some riders also like to carry oil with them, but that's generally a waste of space. Most places have oil.

Attention to the terrain

Select the proper tire for the condition and the terrain that you will be riding. Weather conditions will also affect tire choice. Use heavy duty inner tubes as flat tires always arise on adventure rides. Carry tire changing tools and a small bicycle pump and CO_2 cartridges. Tire selection also depends on the type of terrain. Sometimes there has to be a compromise between traction and mileage. Knobby tires do not last on long distance trips and not all remote places have tires available for replacement. Universal tires give longer range but compromise the bike on the dirt trails. Arrange for a set of replacement tires at a local shop or ship them to where you are staying. Know what terrain to expect to help balance your tire choice.

Know who you are riding with

Riding with someone new can be dangerous because you do not know his or her riding style, skill level and common sense. This will affect how the trip is planned. A novice rider may be adequate on the flats and simple trails, but when the group approaches a steep descent covered with rocks, a more experienced rider will have to help that rider through the obstacle. If you are going to bring them, be prepared to assist the novice rider.

Organized trail rides

There are group adventure rides available, such as the Nevada Rally Experience, organized by Scot Harden and Casey Folks. NRE is a 500 mile organized trail ride over three days. A road book is handed out to each rider and discussed in detail. The ride starts in the desert (elevation 2000 feet) and quickly turns into trails and sand

The best adventure rides are often shared amongst good friends. (Photo by Scott Cox.)

The Nevada Rally Experience captures the beauty of adventure riding. (Photo by Stephan Legrand.)

Packing for the ride

There are many places to put things on adventure bikes: over the gas tank, under the seat, on the silencer brace, in the side compartments, rear container, fanny pack, back pack and riding jacket to name a few. First, assess everyone's needs and plan accordingly. The basic principle is to share the load. For example, one guy brings the camping gear and the other brings the food, jumper cables, and a volt meter. It is about bringing just what you need and not more, although novice riders carry more than experienced riders because they usually do not have a properly prepared bike and know less about the ride.

washes coursing into the mountains and reaching areas of snow patches (elevation 6000 feet). The NRE is a huge success and a yearly event. Most of all, the NRE illustrates the beauty of adventure riding and all it has to offer. Group adventure rides teach many adventure riding skills in a short period of time.

Careful preparation for an adventure ride can really pay off when one finds a neat place and decides to stay there an extra night or so. Preparation, planning and sharing the load are the secrets to any good adventure ride. Knowing your group and planning a good road book are essential. Most importantly, have fun and remember why you are on an adventure ride and dig deep into the spirit that has led you there. Often, we all are just following our own bliss to discover new ground.

The steep mountain roads of the French Alps are a good example why it is so important to check for changing road and trail conditions. (Photo by Joe Barker.)

Packing other essential items such as food, coffee and utensils can be very challenging. Dry and canned foods are usually sufficient; those with camping experience usually do well. It is important to take a portable stove that works on multiple fuels. There is nothing like riding great trails all day long only to run out of butane at the campground. These types of stoves are available at most outdoor stores.

The subject of drinks such as coffee or tea often arises. Taking a French press for coffee along with a jet boiler makes a nice cup of coffee in the wilderness. A cafetiere (a European type of espresso maker) is also ideal as it uses boiling water forced past coffee grounds to brew coffee.

Single wall tents have been developed in recent years. They weigh only about 1.5 pounds and pack down very small. Other camping supplies depend on the personality of the adventure rider and how much he or she wants to carry. There are many options and looking in camping stores like REI or other sporting goods stores is useful.

Medical matters

Plan for minor medical problems like scrapes and bruises and ask if anyone in the group has medical issues. Since many adventure riders are older, chances are that someone has a medical problem. It is also very useful to know who has medical experience and who may be able to perform basic life support services.

Pack a small bag with medical supplies because during the day the most likely medical events that you will encounter are exhaustion, heat injury or even some form of trauma. Consider taking gauze, medical tape, saline (for washing the eyes), medications like Tylenol and ibuprofen, rubber gloves, your insurance policy and emergency contact numbers.

Research contact information of pharmacies in nearby towns and the name and location of the nearest major hospital. Every rider in the group should have a piece of paper with their age, medical allergies, medical history, past surgeries, medications, and insurance information. The time this little piece of paper can save may be life saving.

Back up plans

Many times the weather does not turn out to be as predicted or a rider is injured. Having a plan for procedures can make a huge difference for every one in the group. For example, knowing the locations of post offices may help if someone has to abandon the ride. This way, his belongings can be sent home instead of carried by someone else. Carrying a satellite phone on a ride can be invaluable in the event someone has broken down or is injured. Many satellite phone plans charge you only when you use them. Always have back up cash available. Some small towns may not take credit cards and you may have to resort to bartering just to get gas. Study

Helping each other over obstacles like this fallen tree shows the essence and spirit of adventure riding. (Photo by Jonathan Beck.)

Sharing the experience and riding great distances are one of the many rewards of adventure riding. (Photo by Johnathan Edwards.)

Exploring new lands comes with meeting new cultures. (Photo by H. Peuker.)

the culture and types of towns where you are going!

Returning from an adventure ride

Hopefully, you are planning another adventure ride when you return from this one. There are some practical things to do to make the next ride easier.

Always wash the bike, check the bolts and wheels, oil the chain and moving parts. Note the wear on the moving parts such as the chain and sprockets. Make notes of the highlights and difficulties of the trip as soon as possible to better plan for the next adventure ride. Special things to pay attention to are dirt roads and washes

Adventure riding is as popular in Europe as it is in North America. (Photo by Joe Barker.)

that did not exist on the map, cattle crossings and ranches, gas stops and of course what

problems and adventures you encountered.

On the next page is a list of possible items to take along on an adventure ride. The categories are separated into clothing, riding gear, personal, tool / spares, accessories, cooking, camping, motorcycle and miscellaneous. It's not a fully comprehensive list. One needs to pick and choose and add items as necessary, according to the particular needs of the ride and your machine.

Clothing	Road Riding gear	Personal	Tools / Spares	Accessories
Bandanna	Down vest	Batteries	Butane solder iron	Belt/fanny pack
Belt	Ear plugs	Cell/Satellite phone	Electric wire	Cargo net
Fleece pants	Gloves	Chargers	Grey tape	Day pack
Fleece shorts	Goggles	Copies	JB Weld epoxy	Face shield cleaner
Fleece hat	Gortex boots	Credit cards	Jumper cables	First aid kit
Jeans	Helmet & dark shield	Digital cameras	Ohm meter	G.P.S.
Long John's	Jacket liner	Electric shaver	Plastic ties	Helmet lock cable
Long sleeve shirt	Leather riding pants	Lip balm	Safety wire	Hi-lighter markers
Shorts	Rain gear	Medicines	Siphon hose	Maps
Shower sandals	Kidney belt	Passport / Visa	Socket set	Music device
Sneakers	Ski mask	Money	Spare tubes	Pen and journal
Turtle neck shirt	Vest	Sunglasses	Spark plug	
Tee shirts	Dirt riding gear	Sunscreen	Standard tool kit	
	Chest protector	Toiletries	Tie straps	
	Jerseys	Towel	Tire gauge	
	Pads / bike shorts	Wallet	Tire irons	
	Riding boots	Wet ones	Tow strap	
			Tube patch kit	
			Vise grips	

Cooking	Motorcycle	Camping	Miscellaneous
Coffee maker	Cable lock	Alarm	Batteries & memory cards
Coffee & filters	Disc lock	Bivouac bag	(for digital cameras)
Candles	Cycle cover	Candle lantern	Dictionaries (foreign)
Cups / Bottles	Insurance copy	Chair	Energy drinks
Espresso maker	M/C manual	Flashlight	Leatherman
Flares	Registration	Ground cloth	Pepper spray
Gas stove	Spare keys	Pillow	Trail pack
Instant coffee	Tank bag	Relief bottle	Tank packs
Instant meals	Oils / lubricants	Sleeping bag	Vacuum packs
Lighter (disposable)	Chain lube	Stakes	Zip ties / bags
Oatmeal	Contact cleaner	Tent	
Plates	Filter oil		
Snack bars	Funnel		
Spices	Grease		
Tea bags			
Utensils			

Table by Joe Barker

Chapter 10

STRATEGIES FOR RALLY RACING

A bend in the road is not the end of the road … unless you fail to make the turn.

Photo by Maindruphoto.

The Dakar Rally—it is everything one hopes for and everything one fears. Finishing the rally comes with a tremendous sense of personal satisfaction and relief. The emotion of that moment is never forgotten. What one most remembers is the intense character of the rally. A band of brotherhood is formed for life from what has been accomplished; the best memories of the rally are the fight and camaraderie that ties everyone together as a team. The following is an excerpt taken from Scot Harden's personal journal:

No other rally racer lent more moral or technical support or was a better friend to the KTM Red Bull U.S. effort than Alfie Cox. The man was rock solid in his support, not to mention he kept us all laughing like hell throughout the event. Alfie Cox is a prince among men and a true sportsman and gentleman of the desert.

Racing the Dakar Rally has changed greatly in the recent years. The depth of the riding talent has expanded dramatically. Historically, at any given time there have been three to five riders who could run the lead pace. Nowadays, on any given stage there are almost fifteen riders who roll out and put it to the lock for the next ten to twelve hours. The pace has certainly picked up and the battle for stage wins is much more intense. This is another reason the margin for safety is shrinking. Fifteen riders pushing each other very hard each day adds to the pressure. Add to this the fact that they are all more or

KTM Red Bull rider Chris Blais in the opening stage of the 2006 Dakar Rally. (Photo by DPPI.)

Many different cultures and customs are encountered during the Dakar rally. (Photo by Johnathan Edwards.)

Channel" devoted a half-hour per day to the event before being outbid by Outdoor Life Network for 2005. Unfortunately, OLN programmed only a single hour-long retrospective well after the event concluded. But for 2006, it has upped its coverage to half-hour long nightly stage recaps, including reporters traveling in the bivouacs, and is working to reach out to a broader segment of the American audience. Hopefully, OLN will build up the American interest for the Dakar Rally as they did for Tour de France.

Some of the Americans involved in the Dakar Rally effort are KTM Red Bull riders Chris Blais, Andy Grider and Kellon Walch. Chris' top three finishes in the final stages and Kellon's win in the final stage were highlights of the 2005 Dakar

less mounted on the same machines, which are very reliable and rarely break. This translates into even more pressure on the riders.

The Dakar Rally is heavily televised in Europe as well as in Japan. Coverage of the race in the United States has been mediocre over the years. In 2003 and 2004, the "Speed

2006 Dakar champion Marc Coma posing with the president of Senegal, Mr. Wade. (Photo by Johnathan Edwards.)

The Dakar Rider Search Challenge was featured on OLN in 2004. It was used to develop an American team for victory in Dakar. From left to right are Andy Griders, Chris Blais, Kellon Walch, Scot Harden, Casey McCoy, Jonah Street and Kenny Bartram. (Photo by Mark Kariya.)

The Dakar rally is very heavily televised in over 30 different countries. (Photos by Johnathan Edwards.)

Rally. Andy and Chris repeated top finishes in the 2006 rally, with Chris Blais finishing fourth overall. American privateer Jonah Street finished second and third in the later stages. Blais, Grider and Walch were chosen from a reality television show called the Dakar Challenge Rider Search, which took place in Death Valley, California. The show was featured on OLN in 2004.

Participation of American privateers has recently increased. Privateers like David and Charlie Rauseo and James Embro are the epitome of the Dakar Rally experience. They endured three grueling weeks with some of the toughest sand dunes ever introduced in the Dakar Rally, but they always had smiles on their faces and never lost site of the goal. David crashed near the end and injured his foot, and afterward it looked like it should have been amputated. No one could believe that he road through so much pain.

How the Dakar Rally works

The competitors and their machines arrive in the host city, where technical inspection and the first stage of the rally take place. During technical inspection (or scrutineering), all competitors must take a GPS course, an emergency beacon (balise) class, undergo medical clearance and receive other vital information. The race starts January 1st and consists of a liaison and a short special. Here is some Dakar Rally vocabulary to better understand the process:

Bivouac

This literally means "camp" in French. Bivouacs are always situated at airports and can contain more than 2000 people. Briefings are held at the bivouacs, as well as breakfast and dinner.

Documentation and scrutineering

Every rally starts with a check of participants and bikes. All team members must be accredited and all bikes must comply with the rules of the Fédération Internationale de Motocyclisme (FIM).

Parc Ferme

After scrutineering, the bikes have to go into parc fermé, a closed area where they cannot be touched until the next day just before the start. No one is permitted to enter except the rider, who is only admitted half an hour before his start time.

Parc fermé in Morocco. (Photo by Thorsten Flechsig.)

This is to avoid modifications being done to bikes after the technical scrutineering.

Prologue

The prologue is a first short special test defining the starting order for the first stage. The time of the prologue counts toward the general result.

Liaison

A liaison is the route to, between or after special stages; it may be on or off-road. The

These boxes, called "canteens," are transported by airplane to each bivouac during the Rally and are used to store clothes, supplies and personal items. But for privateers, it is their world for three weeks. (Photo by Johnathan Edwards.)

riders have a maximum time to go to the next check point, and are penalized if they exceed that time for whatever reason. The time of the liaison does not count for the final result. Liaisons range from 50 to 500 kilometers.

Special Test

The special test is a stage of the race that times the competitors from start to the finish; the Dakar Rally resembles the Tour De France in this manner. The final result is made up by the addition of the times of the special stages, plus penalties for exceeding liaison times or missing check points.

Check Point (CP)

A special test is equipped with several check points where the riders receive a stamp on their time cards. The check points prove that a rider is on the right track and on time.

Road book

Each day the riders receive a road book which indicates the route of the day. The information in a road book consists of pictures with arrows and quick information (e.g. Danger!!!), as well as the distance to the information on the next picture and the overall distance.

GPS

A GPS device used with the road book so riders can find their way through the course. The organizers set waypoints in every stage which are recorded in the road book. Riders have to pass them correctly or be penalized.

Competitors are required to attend classes during scrutineering prior to the start of the Dakar rally. (Photo by Johnathan Edwards.)

Selecting a Dakar Rally bike

Preparation for the Dakar Rally is a culmination of over a year of planning. Participation in the rally is 70 percent preparation and 30 percent actual performance. Without successful preparation, it is unlikely a rider will reach Dakar. Countless hours of training (both physical and mental),

The XT Yamaha 500 is an example of a vintage bike entry in the Dakar rally. And this motorcycle did make it to Dakar. (Photo by Johnathan Edwards.)

logistical concerns, motorcycle fabrication and communication are required, all for the journey of a lifetime.

In recent years, the evolution of the rally motorcycle has advanced tremendously. Compasses have been replaced by GPS, road books are advanced electronically, motor-cycles must have water reservoirs and steering stabilizers, inner tubes have been replaced by mousse inserts, and the list continues.

Three basic criteria for selecting a Dakar Rally bike are: an overall winning rally bike, adventurer/finishing rally bike, and an exotic entry rally bike.

An overall winning rally bike has a large displacement

engine and may put out 75 horsepower or more. These motorcycles have the latest suspension technology, motor modifications for increased reliability, and weigh less with the addition of carbon fiber, titanium and aluminum parts. These bikes are usually hand built at the factory and are reserved for top professionals who are expected to win.

Adventurer rally race bikes are hybrids of the bikes available to the public. They are custom outfitted to compete in long distance events. The addition of long range fuel tanks, oil coolers and added electrical components are some examples of these modifications. Lighter weight, maneuverability, and cost are

some advantages of these machines in a rally. Additionally, these bikes may be more advantageous in certain stages that have a lot of tight single track or rocks. However, less reliability of the lighter components, slower top speeds and absence of factory support are some of the disadvantages.

An exotic entry rally bike is usually a quad or side car motorcycle. Even Vespas have been entered in the Dakar Rally! Exotics are custom built with personalities of their own. These bikes sometimes finish the rally, but often break down during the sand dune stages which are very hard on the engine.

Whatever motorcycle is used for the Dakar Rally, it is imperative that the machine be custom fit to the rider. The rider must be comfortable with the use and location of his or her navigational instruments. Some advantage can be gained by using the new Speeddox / CAP repeater. This instrument duplicates the CAP heading and warns the rider of speed infractions. Often the Dakar Rally rider must make decisions with confidence to maintain the correct path. For the mid pack rider, following tracks is not always the best policy.

The race itself

The riders gear up for an early depart from the bivouac; they ride the liaison and arrive to the start of the special test. This is where most of the

Rule and regulations are very strict during the Dakar Rally; here Claudia Palmer, Team manager of KTM Gauloises and Patrick Zaniroli, 2005 Dakar rally race director, talk about rules and penalties during the Dakar rally. (Photo by Johnathan Edwards.)

intense riding takes place—sand dunes, high speed straights, and rocks.

Most special tests range from 50 to 350 kilometers and when finished, the competitors must return to the bivouac via another liaison. Once back to the bivouac, the riders hand in their time cards and pick up a new road book. Then they take a rest, give the motorcycle to the mechanics, and try to replenish themselves by drinking fluids and eating. Most amateurs do not have their own mechanics, so they must maintain their own motorcycles.

After dinner, the evening briefing takes place. The briefing is always in French, and a translator is present for those who do not speak the language. At the briefing, all the dangers and exceptions of the next stage are revealed, and

penalties and awards are given out. Penalties result from speeding through villages, going off the course (hors piste), or missing a check point. The rules for the Dakar Rally are very strict. This makes sense considering the safety

measures required to keep some 600 competitors from many different countries out of trouble as they race through Europe and Africa.

Following the briefing and after reviewing their road books, the competitors must try to sleep in their tents while generators, air tools and wind continue to make noise throughout the night. Since sleeping is often difficult and the start for motorcycles is often as early as 3 A.M, sleep deprivation is a huge factor during the rally.

This cycle of events continues for three weeks. The Dakar Rally is not about going as fast as you can each stage. The race to Lac Rose (the Pink Lake) is very long and one must employ a smooth, efficient technique. The rally can be many things, including punishing as well as rewarding, but most of

Chris Blais passes through a village in Senegal. (Photo by DPPI.)

all it is a challenge to the human spirit.

Preparing for the Dakar Rally: with all thy getting, get knowledge

Saint Thomas Moore described Utopia as the ideal world. If a rally rider were to prepare for the Dakar Rally in Utopia, the scheme would run something like this:

When the Dakar Rally is finished, usually some three weeks after the New Year, rally riders say to themselves, "Oh my gosh, how cool would it be to race the Dakar Rally and be a part of the legend!" Realize that when the rally is finished, the official announcer, Toby Moody, inevitably quips in his ironic English accent, "See you in eleven months." Eleven months! Yes, after the rally is finished you now have eleven months to prepare, train, gather finances and sponsors, as well as explain to your wife why you are going to be away in Africa for over a month!

In Utopia, the eager rally racer would prepare for Dakar something like this: Upon waking up from his dream of winning the stage from Atar to Bamako, he is served a nutritious breakfast while reading over his road book and GPS coordinates. He starts his training with a light 3 mile jog. Later, he takes the rally bike and practices on the giant sand dunes located nearby. Of

KTM Red Bull rider Andy Grider finished second overall in this stage of the 2006 Dakar Rally. (Photo by DPPI.)

course, a mechanic in an assistance vehicle chases. In the sand the rally racer practices dropping and lifting the rally bike five times in succession and lets his heart rate climb up to 180 or 190 beats per minute.

He then continues on to a predetermined spot where a mini-bivouac is set up. Here he has lunch while he tosses the bike to the mechanics with an unlimited supply of parts. Afterwards, the team doctor looks him over and gives him a lightly chilled sport drink and energy bar.

The rally racer in Utopia rides to another challenging pre-marked GPS course full of rocks and blazing fast trails. After another 200 miles, he returns home, leaving the bike in the garage where the mechanic preps it again for the next ride.

The rider then replenishes himself with another electrolyte drink and sports bar followed by a massage from the team doctor to ease his aching muscles while listening to pleasant Dakar music from Senegalese singer Youss'n Dour.

After his massage, the rally rider heads off on his bicycle for 30 or 40 miles in beautiful countryside, accompanied, of course, by famous cyclists who just happen to live in the same town. Then he goes to the gym and does a round of circuit training, working the upper body and legs, followed by complex proprioception training exercises to improve his balance and ending with a stretching routine.

Riding the rally bike back to the house, the racer sees some young kids who want his autograph. He chats with

Factory Red Bull KTM rider Chris Blais finished an amazing 4th overall in the Dakar 2006 rally. (Photo by DPPI.)

them for a few minutes and encourages them in the sport, then returns to the house to spend some time with his family on a pleasant afternoon drive.

Does the rally training in Utopia stop here? Golly gee, no! As he drives, the rally rider pops his favorite French lesson into the CD and starts repeating back complex French sentences with perfect pronunciation, asking to fill up his gas tank and ending with *s'il vous plait*.

After dinner, the whole family gathers around the nice plasma screen TV to watch previous editions of the Rally (with Toby Moody announcing) to study lines and terrain that will surely appear in the next Dakar Rally. Finally, the rally racer in Utopia kisses his wife good night as he heads out to his tent in the back yard where there is an air cargo box full of the necessities for the

next day—already prepared, of course.

Realistically preparing for Dakar

Now for a dose of reality: starting from the idea of competing in the event to financing your entry is a monumental task. Here are some basic issues everyone has to deal with:

Do you need to be able to speak French?

No, it is not a requirement. It is, however, an advantage. The Dakar Rally is a French organized event. The company is called A.S.O., or Amaury Sport Organization. Many of the Dakar Rally staff speak English. Road books are available in French or English, but you will

The nightly briefing (always in French) is very important as changes in the road book are announced, as well as awards and penalties. (Photo by Johnathan Edwards.)

find some of the English instructions are acronyms based on French words. For example "G" on your road book means "left" for the French word *gauche*, while "D" means right for the French word *droite*. The nightly briefings are in French; English interpretation is provided through headsets. Each country through which the rally passes is mainly French-speaking. Some advice: expect French politics.

How does the GPS work?

The GPS is a limited capability GPS, which means only certain information is available to the competitor. The A.S.O. provides some basic GPS training for all riders during scrutineering or technical inspection. If you have never used a GPS, some advance training is recommended, or take an adventure riding school that teaches navigation techniques.

What riding skill level is required?

This depends on your goals and expectations. Naturally, a professional level is required to win the Dakar Rally. Simply finishing, however, requires adequate preparation and an intermediate to advanced skill level. There is a good chance you will crash. This is another reason fitness is important. It is also important to have top of the line protective gear. It is a long race with many surprises.

Desert rally training – how should you prepare?

If you have little dune or desert rally experience, going to a training camp provided by desert rally experts is highly recommended. Many schools are available from world class experts such as Scot Harden, Jimmy Lewis, Jordi Acarons and Alfie Cox. In a desert rally, one must be able to effectively read the terrain, operate the bike, navigate and use the GPS and road book all at the same time. The Dakar Rally is not the place to learn this. Ride the motorcycle many hours; get used to riding for ten hours straight. Anticipate that your reaction times will decrease, so be careful. Concentrate on

sand, as the dunes often are the hardest obstacle in the rally.

What goals are realistic for a first time Dakar participant?

For entry level riders, we suggest setting a realistic goal of finishing. This means pacing yourself so you don't burn up all of the energy today that you may need tomorrow.

What medical tests and supplies are needed?

A medical clearance must be obtained by all participants. If you are over 50 years old you will also need a cardiac stress test. Malaria prevention is paramount. Most participants take Malarone or Larium; consult your medical physician

Bivouac Medical Kit

Imodium—stops diarrhea effectively

Ciprofloxacin 500mg tablets—effective in curing/ avoiding diarrhea or stomach problems if a single pill is taken as early as possible

Ibuprofen or Diclofenac tablets—great for pain, sprains and strains

Chloramphenicol eye drops—for conjunctivitis (eye infection).

Powder electrolytes— oral rehydration powder

Anti-fungal foot cream— for itch / athletes foot

Deep Heat—smells great and feels good on sore muscles

Betadine Spray—great on any abrasions or cuts

before taking these medications. A yellow fever vaccine is required for entry into certain countries; also, Hepatitis A, B and other standard immunizations are helpful.

What medical support is available?

The Dakar Rally is equipped with a mobile medical hospital at each bivouac. Participants may receive medications for various ailments, treatment for cuts and bruises, and even an x-ray if

The Dakar rally is equipped with a mobile mini medical hospital capable of fixing minor problems to performing major surgery. (Photo by Johnathan Edwards.)

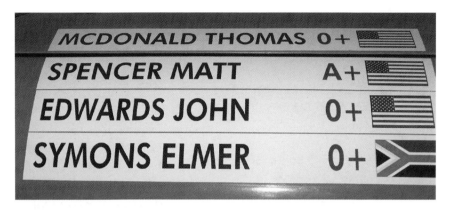

Everyone involved in the Dakar Rally is identified by name and nationality. The blood types indicate the inherent danger of the Rally. (Photo by Johnathan Edwards.)

a broken bone is suspected. Some injuries are flown to a hospital for definitive treatment.

Filling up with gas at check points: It is better to take gas than to ride looking for gas

Charlie Rauseo, an American privateer on the 2005 Dakar Rally, wrote the following in his journal: *Bikes and cars are stuck and broken everywhere. Several times, I nearly ran over groups of riders huddling together under emergency foil blankets in the desert cold. Did I mention the sandstorm and rain? But I just kept going, mostly standing up through the camel grass next to the torn-up track. The going was very, very slow in the dark.*

Charlie is talking about the infamous stage eleven during the 2005 Dakar Rally. It lasted for over 10 hours and consisted of grueling camel grass, dunes and desert roads. Near the end

of the stage only thirty motorcycles were in by nightfall; only ten cars were in by midnight. Many riders were stranded at night in the desert with minimal supplies because they ran out of gas. After check point three, the promoters underestimated the distance to the next check point and limited the amount of fuel to 20 liters per motorcycle. After looking at

the road book, most of the top riders knew that 20 liters would not be enough to reach the next check point. The riders who made it into the bivouac insisted on taking double the gas, despite the protest of the officials at the check point. One privateer said he just took the gas and quietly got back in the line.

As fate would have it, those riders were right to take the extra gas. Over a hundred and thirty bikes were left stranded in the desert that night. Some spent the entire night huddled under their thermal blankets and running out of water. The organization later admitted that there was a miscommunication and that more gas should have been permitted. Nonetheless, many top contenders like Eric Verhoef were stranded and lost hours of

During difficult navigation conditions, riders often stay together to find the way. (Photo by Maindruphoto.)

time, ending any chance of a high finish. Knowing how far your bike can go after filling it with gas is important and can be life saving.

Passing other riders in a rally

For a professional rider, the goal of the Dakar Rally is usually to win. For the majority it is to finish. In order to win the race, it is obligatory to pass other riders. This may seem like a mundane point, but passing is a talent. Much like the Tour de France, the Rally resembles a chess game. Moves must be calculated and well planned. Anyone can ride a motorcycle fast for one day, but to do it for eighteen consecutive days is another feat. Riders must ask themselves many questions before trying to advance in the rally: what is the history of the rider ahead? Is he known to crash? Does he have a history of leading riders astray and then leaving them behind? Richard Sainct was known for leading riders off the path, acting like he had a mechanical, then taking off in the other direction, costing his adversaries valuable time. One thing is for sure in the Dakar Rally...no one is going to win it their first time. The dynamics of the race are far too complicated.

Here is a little more Dakar history. During the 2005 Dakar Rally, Kellon Walch was ready to make his move into the top five and found himself behind Fabrizio Meoni. Kellon decided

Larry Roseler advises that following other riders is often a good strategy to give your mind a rest and to save energy. (Photo by G. Soldano.)

to pass Meoni. However, Meoni was riding slow for a reason and moments later Kellon crashed very hard in the same place a Spanish rider named Jordi Duran crashed.

Kellon ignored a couple of things in this situation. He knew Meoni had a lot more experience, and he should have stayed behind him even if it was for the whole day. There is also a sort hierarchy in the Dakar Rally; you do not just pass everyone at once. Kellon should have shown more respect for Meoni in this situation and waited for a better moment. Passing in a rally must be a well thought out action.

Larry Roseler, a multi Baja 1000 and enduro champion, advises riders in the Dakar Rally to position themselves into groups of experienced riders and follow them until they feel more comfortable

navigating. Once riders are comfortable with GPS navigation and using the road book, they may take turns being the leader. Most of the pressure of navigating is on the leader, taking a tremendous amount of mental energy which adds up day after day. Following, rather than leading, permits riders to relax and take a mental break.

The road book

Each day in the Dakar Rally an official road book is given to all competitors. The road book is a scroll cut to fit on a holder which can be advanced forwards and backwards. Route information such as direction, check points, gas stops, obstacles, GPS way points, kilometers markings, dangerous areas, cap headings, total distance traveled, and distance between GPS points and kilometer markings are marked. The road book provides

Riders can spend up to two hours each night reviewing and editing the next day's road book. (Photo by Johnathan Edwards.)

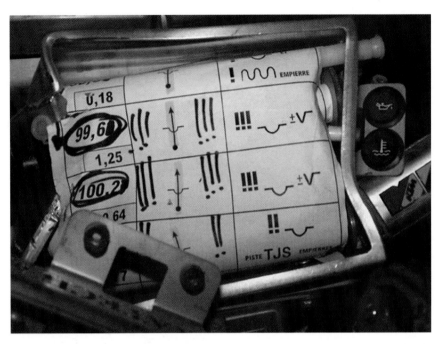

Riders develop highly personalized systems for noting dangers in the road book; sometimes, that is not enough. (Photo by Johnathan Edwards.)

navigational information to be used with the GPS and odometer in order to find the correct route—which is the definition of the word rally.

For some rallies the route information emphasizes speed and driving skill, as well as point-to-point navigation. A road book aids in safe high-speed driving on a competitive section because it indicates every tiny feature of the course so that the rider may plan for it ahead of time.

One reason the Dakar Rally is difficult for motorcycle competitors is because they must navigate and drive at the same time; car drivers have a navigator with them! Navigating while maneuvering a motorcycle takes some practice.

Navigation information will yield only one correct route for the rally, though sometimes the occasional ambiguity may creep in. Organizers check meticulously, however, to ensure that route information is correct. For example, on many events certain areas are marked off as "black spots" or no-go areas. This will usually be where the organizer does not want the rally coming near a village or populated areas.

Realize the road book is often created by someone in a helicopter or in a jeep traveling at much lower speeds than in racing. Furthermore, the course is often marked some months before the rally and it may have changed tremendously over time. Thus, a good rule is to ride the terrain as fast as you would if you did not have a road book; i.e., like a "fast trail ride." Johnny

Campbell, multi winner of the Baja 1000, competed in the Dakar Rally and finished in the top ten overall by "following the road book and riding a fast trail ride."

Have a system of marking the road book dangers and important points. Most competitors use different color highlighters and it takes sometimes an hour or two to complete. Never underestimate the value of a road book. Jordi Acarons, the Spanish team manager for the Dakar Rally, tells each of his riders, "The road book can save your life." Acarons, a 20-year veteran of the Dakar Rally and highly accomplished rally racer from Spain, ensures that each rider understands the difficult sections and highlights important points every night before they go to bed.

Sleeping in the Dakar Rally

Sleep is usually interrupted by the sound of generators, wind and vehicles coming in late to the bivouac. At the bivouacs, the tents are small and the ground is rough. Riders can get enough sleep, but if something goes wrong, such as a mechanical or a fall, a rider may arrive at the bivouac late. The mechanics (or the rider) may have to work on the bike during the night to prepare for the next morning. This could result in as

Tents provide a brief moment of solace for the competitors during the Rally. (Photo by Johnathan Edwards.)

Riders catch a power nap at the bivouac before the assistance crews arrive. (Photo by G. Soldano.)

little as two hours sleep for the rider, meaning that he or she will be riding in a sleep-deprived state the next morning.

The human brain deals with sleep deprivation in two ways. It either stays very awake and alert or it falls asleep deeply; there is little in between during sleep deprivation. But the mind is a mystical thing, and when necessary, a person can stay awake for days at a time, especially during stressful periods. So one must treat somnolence with respect. Knowing yourself is important when dealing with it.

Scientists believe the body and brain can work on 4.5 to 5 hours of sleep per night. The optimum is to sleep 6 hours and nap for 20 minutes in the afternoon. Much of the information on this subject has been gathered from long distance sailing races, as well as ultra marathon runners and other endurance events. Essentially, one must maintain a balance between being tired and totally awake. The reasons for this are to conserve energy, to remain alert enough to deal with navigation and to have enough "mental reserve" to deal with stressful situations.

A rider preparing for the Dakar Rally should practice sleeping more efficiently before the event. For example, sleeping only 5 or 6 hours a night and then taking a short nap may be a good exercise for a rally rider. The goal is to teach the brain to delve deeper into sleep in a short period of time.

The quality of sleep, not the quantity, is what is important. Learning to go into deep sleep fast and efficiently is a learned process and must be practiced.

Strategies to stay awake

When the mind becomes fatigued, the need for sleep is to rest the brain, not necessarily the body. Decreasing mental annoyances will decrease fatigue. For example ear plugs decrease mental fatigue by decreasing the constant sound transmitted to your brain. Riding with wet clothes and being cold increases mental fatigue as does the feeling of riding on an empty tank wondering where the next gas station is.

It is important is to recognize the symptoms of fatigue: repeatedly yawning, nodding head, tendency to close the eyes, indecision over minor issues and difficulty maintaining the desired speed. Studies have shown that sleep can occur spontaneously in sleep deprived states. Just pull over and take a power nap or

Dakar Rally competitors generally ride from sunrise to sunset. (Photo by DPPI.)

use a stimulant to keep awake; do what ever works best for you.

Some effective habits of long distance riders who compete in the "iron butt" rallies, for example, are to not consume any brain stimulants some weeks prior to the event if at all. This is important because the brain becomes habituated to caffeine. Also maintaining proper hydration and nutrition are essential. While riding, eat small snacks like nuts and fruits during the day, instead of large meals.

Consistency

Consistency is the key to safe habitual riding. The brain anticipates less when it is fatigued. Discipline yourself to always make lane changes the same way or slow down to a safe speed and then look at your road book or GPS.

For example, if you are a person who functions very well with coffee each morning then continue as you would normally. You might need to increase your coffee consumption if the previous night was very stressful and allowed for little sleep and you are faced with a full day ahead. Do whatever it takes to stay awake, as that is what is safe for you and for others.

Power naps

Power naps are a valuable tool for minimizing the effects of fatigue and increasing safety. Some say they are more effective than caffeine. A power nap is usually 10 to 20 minutes long. The longer the nap, the more one will wake up with "sleep inertia." Sleep inertia is

when you wake up from a nap temporarily confused, sluggish and have lack of coordination. As you practice power naps, you will experience less sleep inertia. If you are truly falling asleep on the trail, take the nap and keep yourself safe.

Caffeine for off-road riding

What does coffee and caffeine have to do with off-road riding? Most people relate caffeine with those cycling guys in the Tour de France. Caffeine can help you on your ride or race day just as it does for the cycling world. Coffee and similar beverages contain caffeine, the most widely used drug in the United States (aspirin is second). You probably know caffeine increases mental alertness. Do you also know it improves reflex time in muscles, decreases muscle fatigue, and helps breathing in the lungs? So how can all of these things that caffeine does help in motorcycle riding?

Take a typical day of long adventure riding. After lunch you take a siesta and wake up. The others are leaving fast. Still groggy, you rush to put on your gear and ride up to the trail.

NOW HOLD ON A MINUTE! You are on the trail, not completely alert, and then you will attempt to go fast right away. This is a losing situation, and even worse, a big potential for injuries to yourself and

Energy drinks help to keep you mentally alert during tough stretches on the Dakar rally. (Photo by Johnathan Edwards.)

others. What could help to prevent this catastrophe? One thing you can do is to put a little caffeine in your body about twenty to thirty minutes before you leave.

Caffeine will increase your reaction time and alertness, which can help you to get off to a better start and as a result you will be less likely to crash. The idea here is not "load" your body with tons of caffeine, but use just enough to get the job done.

Caffeine is a diuretic (a drug that makes you urinate), but luckily, it is a weak diuretic by medical standards. Actually, drinking fluids alone has a bigger diuretic effect than caffeine. Drinking too much coffee (6 to 10 cups in a day) will give you headaches, insomnia, make you to urinate excessively, and cause your hands to shake. Moderation is the key.

Caffeine comes in many shapes and sizes. The most common is coffee and cappuccino. There is also tea, some sports drinks, and certain types of soda and energy drinks. Coffee has about 250 to 300 milligrams (mg) per 8 oz. cup. Start off with this dose of caffeine and then modify the dose as needed. Tea has about 35 to 100 mg of caffeine (in an 8 oz. cup). It comes in many different flavors and is easy to make. Remember, caffeine and similar herbs affect people in different ways. For example, if you have never had caffeine in your body, caffeine will have a huge effect; but if you have been using caffeine all of your life, then caffeine will affect you less dramatically. If you have any type of heart condition or seizure condition, please consult your physician for advice.

Most sport drinks do not have caffeine in them, but they have herbs. These herbs are ginseng and guarana (also found in some teas) and they have similar effects as caffeine. In fact, ginseng is reported to be about three times as powerful as caffeine. Forty milligrams of guarana and about 30 mg of ginseng will have close to the same effect of a 8 oz. cup of coffee (250 to 300 mg caffeine).

Source	amount *(mg)*
8oz coffee	
Ground/Brewed	100—250
Instant	65—95
2 oz shot espresso	150—200
soda (Mountain Dew)	45—55
tea	35—100
Sport drink (per serving)	
caffeine	0
guarana	40
ginseng	30

Relative amounts of caffeine in caffeine containing beverages.

Chapter 11

SAFETY AND FUTURE OF RALLY RACING

Dakar is a dream only for the strong ~ Fabrizio Meoni

Photo by H. Peuker.

Following your bliss in life sometimes leads full circle. Completing events such as the Dakar Rally or an adventure ride across the North American continent come with great satisfaction, but also a measurable risk. The question comes back to – "what are people willing to do in order to complete their dreams?" Exploring the outer limits of human endurance is inherently dangerous. Fabrizio Meoni was

Meoni in the 2003 Dakar. (Photo by J. Cunha.)

once quoted saying, "If everyone finished Dakar, the dream is over."

Adrenaline is a double negative

The adrenaline has been brewing for some time now and finally the time has come. Imagine a popular trail ride like the Colorado 500 or the Nevada 200. Months in the making, all the necessary arrangements are made, and you finally arrive. The smell of freedom and being around your riding buddies are evident. You are surrounded by some of the legends of off-road riding and friends that you see once a year. You take off on the trail and all of your turns are perfect and the control of the bike is impeccable. Ten minutes later you find yourself on the ground after blowing past a turn that was not well marked and

your wrist hurts. Many thoughts are running through your head, the first of of which is wondering if you can continue to ride. Then comes "how could this happen in the first ten minutes of the first day?" followed by, "do I have to go to the hospital, and how am I going to explain this to my wife and boss?"

Most of us have experienced this frustration during our riding careers. But what really happened? First, most injuries occur in the beginning of a ride because riding is not balanced with the adrenaline. During these times you feel like you are riding flawlessly and in complete control. In fact, riders tend to overcorrect the bike, are often not scanning properly, tend to overshoot corners, and the list continues. Riders also forget to take the corner at the optimal visual apex.

Optimal Visual Apex—Taking outside line gives you the best view of what may be around the corner. (Photo by Johnathan Edwards.)

> **Top Ten Secrets to Riding within Your Envelope**
>
> - Never forget that you are riding a heavy rally bike.
> - Realize the trail is marked for trail riding speed, not race speed.
> - Most injuries occur in the first minutes of a trail ride.
> - Adrenaline is a double negative.
> - Take the time to warm up.
> - Eat the proper nutrition for optimal brain function.
> - Never make a pass that puts another rider in danger.
> - Respect the size and weight of the rally bike.
> - Go with what you know.
> - Utilize the optimal visual apex.

The optimal visual apex

Generally, most people take corners in such a way that sets them up best for the next corner. On the trails, there is often oncoming traffic. The idea of the optimal visual apex is to enter and exit the corner as to give the best view of an oncoming motorcycle or a huge rock after the corner. This concept is often taught in motorcycle safety schools.

Ride within your envelope

To avoid early morning adrenaline rush accidents, several strategies are at your disposal. First, ride within your means. Never let adrenaline trick you into riding over your ability level. You may ride like this for a while, until it catches up with you. When you ride with adrenaline your scanning abilities for obstacles on the trail are compromised. In fact, most riders perform better during the latter part of a trail ride. Take the time to warm up and give your brain the proper nutrients for clear thinking. Remember, the ride is supposed to be fun; treat it as such. A good rule is to ride at medium pace for at least half an hour. This will allow you to warm up and then you can consider increasing the pace.

The dangers of somnolence and sleep deprivation

Sleep deprivation is a reality on the Dakar Rally as well as adventure rides. Sleep deprivation usually begins about the fourth or fifth day of riding 600 mile stages. Most factory riders go to sleep around 10 P.M. and then wake up between three a.m. to 6 A.M. to leave for the next stage.

The Italian rider story

To illustrate the dangers of sleep deprivation, here are some actual events recorded in the medical journal of the KTM Red Bull Rally team:

During the second to the last stage, at the border of Mauritania and Senegal, I was with the mechanics and Marc Coma. We were at the gas station, and the riders had just completed the special. A motorcycle passed by and a car was turning onto the road. Suddenly, there was a loud thump, and we promptly saw a pair of boots in the sky and a totaled motorcycle.

We rushed to the rider, who was lying on the ground, his right wrist obviously broken and deformed. He was confused and tried to stand up, then collapsed immediately. We attempted to keep him still while I examined his medical situation. I was very concerned he could have had internal bleeding along with severe dehydration.

During this time, a riot had broken out and some of the locals were trying to take things from the bike and even from his jacket. We transported the rider on a sand board into the shade. I started an intra-venous line and gave over two liters of fluids to overcome severe dehydration. Thankfully he came to his senses. The rider turned out to be a 10 year veteran of the Dakar Rally from Italy.

Why was this rider unable to avoid the car?

Sleep deprivation was the main factor why this rider was unable to react to the car. He lacked mental focus as we were near the end of the rally and he had just finished the special test and was on the liaison (transfer section) portion of the stage. Chris Blais says that the liaisons are often more mentally draining and dangerous than the special

An example of the intense fatigue during the Dakar Rally. (Photo by DPPI.)

tests. "When you are racing, you have adrenaline and you are paying attention," he explains. "But on the transfer sections you are doing everything you can just to stay awake. I cannot count how many times I almost rode off the highway!" Furthermore during transfer sections, the road is flat and there are oncoming cars and pedestrians and animals.

Severe dehydration was another factor in this case. The Italian rider was drinking only water instead of a glucose electrolyte replacement drink. As a result, his sodium levels were low and this causes further mental fatigue. The importance of replacing electrolytes cannot be under estimated. Accidents such as this one can be prevented. The rally is mentally draining and one must do everything possible to prevent mental fatigue.

Fallen heroes

The other part of this chapter is devoted to those among us who have fallen chasing their dreams. As risk is inherent in our sport, losing riders is a reality and we have the potential to face unfortunate situations in our riding careers.

KTM lost two of its best rally pilots, Fabrizio Meoni and Richard Sainct, within a year. During the 2005 Dakar Rally, Fabrizio Meoni was in a serious crash between Atar and Kiffa. Despite immediate medical attention, it was not possible to save his life and Fabrizio died of his injuries at the scene of the accident. Some months earlier, Richard Sainct lost his life in a similar crash in the Rally of Egypt. Another factory KTM rider, Andy Caldecott, crashed during the 2006 Dakar Rally. Ironically, he died in the same stretch of Africa that took the life of Fabrizio Meoni.

Fabrizio Meoni

Fabrizio Meoni was born December 31, 1957 and lived in Castiglion Fiorentino, Italy. He was an Italian off-road and endurance motorcycle rider, and a member of the KTM Factory Team. For years Fabrizio Meoni

As villages become more numerous, riders must exercise more caution (Photo by G. Soldano.)

Meoni in the Dakar Rally, 2003. (Photo by J. Cunha.)

Fabrizio Meoni helps Scot Harden and Joe Barker with the road book and GPS. (Photo by Thorsten Flechsig.)

had a formative influence on rally racing. Twice—in 2001 and 2002—he won the toughest rally in the world. He departed for yet another Dakar Rally on New Year's Eve, 2004—his 47th birthday. During an earlier rally he had promised his family to stop racing altogether so that he could spend more time with his wife and his two children. But he could not resist the excitement and pain—rally racing was his absolute passion. Unfortunately, the 2005 Dakar Rally was to be his last. He was killed January 11 in Kiffa, Mauritania.

For most, just being next to Meoni was like being next to electricity. He represented pure passion and commitment to rally racing; words cannot justify his character. Like Richard Sainct, Meoni knew the road book better than anyone and that is one reason why his death is so hard to accept.

Fabrizio symbolized the ideal racing driver. Most will always remember his birthday on New Year's Eve in Barcelona. The room was full of balloons and he burst all of them. He was just like a little boy. One wasn't enough for him—he had to burst them all.

Fabrizio personified the Dakar Rally; he lived it. Everyone looked up to him. Always searching for challenges, he wasn't satisfied with the simple, and he always wanted to fight. One team manager recalled, "He was such a nice guy, a friend. Fabrizio was a true Italian, one who knew how to live."

For many he was a hero; it was incredible to see someone who was 47 years of age in such fantastic physical condition and in such high spirits. Fabrizio was a great motorcycle rider and an extraordinary man. He

Meoni shows his game face before a stage in the 2004 Rally. (Photo by H. Peuker.)

Sainct and Meoni celebrate podium finishes in Dakar. (Photo by J. Cunha.)

was always open-minded and honest. Anyone who knew him just had to like him.

Richard Sainct

Richard Sainct (April 14, 1970 - September 29, 2004), a native of Saint Affrique, France, began his racing career in enduro and then led into rally racing. He had won the Dakar rally three times. His other notable achievements include winning the Tunisia Rally twice, in 1998 and 1999; the Moroccan Rally in 1997, 1998, 2001 and 2002, and the Rally of Egypt in 2002. He also won the FIA Rally Raid World Cup in 2002.

Richard was another fierce competitor in rally racing, but his mild mannered personality could lead others to believe otherwise. He raced with a cunning ability and at times he would lead his competitors astray from the course, pretending as if he had a mechanical problem, and then he would take the correct route. Although he was known for his trickery, he rarely had to use them because he was usually far ahead of the competition in

Richard Sainct full throttle up a sandy incline. (Photo by Pierro Batini.)

Richard Sainct during the 2004 Tunisia test. (Photo by H. Peuker.)

Andy Caldecott during the 2006 Dakar Rally. (Photo by Pierro Batini.)

to the limit, he was known for his easy going manner and humility.

The deaths of these riders are a testament to the dangers of the race. As KTM's Heinz Kinigardner remarked, "The Dakar Rally is certainly no walk in the park."

Safety and cervical spine protection

any case. He was also known for certain jokes like removing the gear shift lever from of his friends' bikes before a ride.

Andy Caldecott

Andy Caldecott also died chasing his dream. He was born in Keith, South Australia on August 10, 1964 and won the

Australian Safari Rally four times consecutively (2001-2004). He competed in the Dakar Rally in 2004 and 2005, and again in 2006 when he was killed on January 9th, 250 km into the 599 km special stage from Nouakchott to Kiffa, during the 9th stage of rally. Caldecott won stages of the rally and even though he pushed himself

Meoni, Sainct and Caldecott all suffered cervical neck injuries. Effective protection of the neck does not really exist, particularly in the case of the motorcyclist. New safety equipment is being developed for motorcycle riding al the time. For example, a neck brace developed by Chris Leatt, M.D., a South African neurosurgeon, may help prevent neck injuries during a crash. The brace contours the helmet and during the crash helps to transfer the forces from the neck to other parts of the body. This may decrease injuries to the neck. Although

Andy Caldecott rides with perfect form in the sands of Mauritania. (Photo by DPPI.)

Neck braces such as these may revolutionize rally and adventure riding. (Photo by Stephan Legrand.)

Fabrizio Meoni Testing in Tunisia in 2004. (Photo by H. Peuker.)

Rally racers such as Chris Blais and Cyril Despres use this brace during rally competition. (Photo by Stephan Legrand.)

more research is needed in the prevention of injuries during motorcycle riding, neck braces such as these are a step in the right direction.

Safety and the Dakar Rally

The safety of the Dakar Rally has always been challenged by the media, even as the organizers try constantly to ensure the safety of the competitors. The very nature of the sport, however, is inherently dangerous. When chasing the dream of Dakar, riders must fully

prepare themselves to complete the journey as safely as possible. The physical and mental preparation must not be taken lightly.

A number of factors must be considered in the interest of safety, particularly for motorcycles. First, distances between checkpoints and refueling should be examined. In 2005, A.S.O. regulations required motorcycles to carry almost 45 liters (112 pounds) of fuel. Most accidents happen after refueling when the bike is laden with full tanks. Riding a rally machine at speed in these conditions leaves little margin for error. There is just no way to pitch the bike to one side or another because it is so heavy and the velocity is so high. Andy Caldecott, Fabrizio Meoni and Richard Sainct all crashed shortly after refueling.

Secondly, the road book and GPS navigation systems should be redesigned with rider safety in mind. Their mounting position on the bike puts them in an ideal place to damage the upper body and head in the event of a crash. Chris Blais and Scot Harden will tell you that the road book will knock you out just while you ride along! Certainly, some type of padding to the road book needs to be added or some device worn to blunt the impact in the event of a crash.

Third, the organization should have at least one motorcyclist involved in making the road book. Currently, road books are created by someone marking the course from a jeep or a helicopter. Notations for dangers and other hazards look different traveling at 20 mph versus 70 mph.

We must never forget the inherent danger that comes with following our bliss in life, whether it is chasing a rally or completing a new adventure ride across the mountains. The machines we ride are agile, but very unforgiving. Always ride a rally bike with the respect she deserves.

God speed to all of those who have fallen chasing their dream.

Chapter 12

LIST OF MANUFACTURERS AND SERVICE PROVIDERS

Action Products, Inc.
Make pressure relieving products for medical and sports (the gel works well in motorcycle seats)
www.actionproducts.com

Adventure Rider
Information and chat site for the adventure rider
www.advrider.com

Aerostich Riderwear
Clothing and accessories for motorcycle gear
www.aerostich.com

Alpinestars
Motorcycle boots
www.alpinestars.com

Amary Sport Organisation
www.Dakar.com

American Motorcyclist Association
www.ama-cycle.org

Arai
Motorcycle helmets
www.arai.com

Baja Designs
Off-road lighting systems and accessories
www.bajadesigns.com

Best In The Desert Racing Association
Off road desert racing organization / Casey Folks
www.bitd.com

Blais Racing Services
Race bike preparation and accessories
www.blaisracingservices.com

Champion Nutrition
Sports Nutrition and supplements
www.champion-nutrition.com

Delorme
Street atlas USA GPS mapping software
www.delorme.com

Dunlop Tires
www.dunlopmotorcycle.com

FMF
Motorcycle exhaust pipes
www.fmfracing.com

KTM Adventure Tours
Adventure rides and instruction
www.ktmadventuretours.com

Garmin Corporation
GPS and navigation equipment
www.garmin.com

Gerbing's Heated Clothing
Electronically heated clothing
www.gerbing.com

Harden Off Road
Adventure riding information and racing services by Scot Harden
www.harden-offroad.com

Internet BMW Riders
BMW motorcycling club with information about BMW motorcycles
www.ibmwr.org

IMS
Off road parts and accessories
www.imsproducts.com

Jimmy Lewis Racing
Adventure rider training and rally schools
www.jimmylewisracing.com

KTM Hard Equipment
Motorcycle gear and protection
www.ktm.com

LDComfort
Seamless underwear
www.ldcomfort.com

Malcolm Smith Motorsports
www.malcolmsmith.com

Malcolm Smith Racing
Motorcycle gear and protection
www.msroffroad.com

Metzeler Tires
www.metzelermoto.com

Michelin Tires
www.two-wheels.michelin.com

Motion Pro
Motorcycle tools and accessories
www.motionpro.com

Motoport
Weatherproof motorcycle gear
www.motoport.com

Motorcycle Safety Foundation
Motorcycle training classes
www.msf-usa.org

Motorex Oils
www.motorex.net

Neveu Pelletier Organisation
Organizers for the Moroccan and Tunisian rallies
www.NPOlive.com

Ogio equipment
Gear bags, back packs, etc.
www.ogio.com

Performance Bike
Mainly bicycle accessories with some items applicable to adventure riding (e.g. hand pumps)
www.perfomancebike.com

PIAA
Off road motorcycle lighting systems
www.piaa.com

Precision Concepts
Suspension and motor modifications for motorcycles
www.precisionconcepts.com

Pro Vue Goggle Systems
Prescription goggle lens
www.pro-vue.com

Progressive Suspension
Suspension modification for off road motoryles
www.progressivesuspension.com

REI
Outdoor camping and adventure rider accessories
www.rei.com

RK Excel chains
http://www.rk-excel.co

Score International
Organizers of the Baja 1000
www.score-international.com

Shoei
Motorcycle helmets
www.shoei.com

Sidi Sport
Italian made motorcycle gear and apparel
www.sidisport.com

Smartwool
Wool socks and warm weather gear
www.smartwool.com

Smith Sport Optics
Goggles and eyewear for off-road riding
www.smithsport.com

Stanford University Sleep Center
Information about sleep deprivation
www.aaafoundation.org

Stretching by Bob Anderson
A very practical stretching manual
www.shelterpub.com

The Earplug Company
Custom fitted ear plugs
www.earplugco.com

Touratech
German maker of motorcycle accessories for adventure riding (road books, rally computers and luggage systems.
www.touratech-usa.com

Walter Reed Army Institute of Research
A research experiment of sleep deprived soldiers in combat
www.usafa.af.mil

White Power Suspension
Suspension for motorcycles
www.wpsuspension.com

Whitehorse Press
Motorcycle related books, videos and accessories
www.whitehorsepress.com

United States Department of Transportation
A web site of US scenic highways and byways
www.byways.org

United States National Park Service
Information about parks and monuments in the USA
www.nps.gov

Interesting off road and adventure riding websites:

Alaska Rider Tours
www.akrider.com

Chris Blais—KTM Red Bull rally racer
www.blaisracing.com

Charlie Rauseo—Veteran Dakar Rally privateeer
www.charliedakar.com

Source for motorcycle media
www.dualsportmotorcycling.com/stories.htm

Andy Grider—KTM Red Bull rally racer
www.griderracing.com

Jimmy Lewis Off-Road
www.jimmylewisoffroad.com

Kellon Walch—KTM Red Bull rally racer
www.kellonwalch.com

Set ups for KLR, suspension mods
www.klr650.cc/

Adventure riding news
www.ktmtalk.com

Chris Leatt, M.D.
www.leatt-brace.com

MAP Engineering
www.map-engineering.com

On-line motorycycle magazine
www.onewheeldrive.net

Rider Valley
www.rvmc.com

Russell Saddles
www.day-long.com

If you are having trouble finding someone to go on an adventure ride, just look on the web and go to:

www.dualsportnews.com/ridebuddies.html

You can submit your name and the type of ride you are proposing and find a mate!

GLOSSARY

Terms commonly encountered on the Dakar Rally.

AG. An abbreviation for "à gauche," meaning "go left."

AD. *A droite,* meaning to go right.

ASO. This is an abbreviation for the Organization of the Dakar Rally, officially the Amaury Sport Organization. Originally, the organizer was the Thierry Sabine Organization (TSO), named after Thierry Sabine, the rally's founder. After Thierry's death, Thierry's father Gilbert took over, and when he retired, he sold his rights to the ASO. The ASO also organizes the popular cycling race called the Tour de France.

Assistance vehicles. These go from bivouac to bivouac to support the competition vehicles, and are used mainly to carry managers, mechanics and others.

Balise. A balise (or beacon) is an emergency-use rescue signal transmitter, which every participant is required to carry. It can also be used as a desert landmark (air route marker).

Bivouac. A French word literally meaning "camp." More than 2,000 people participate in the Dakar Rally, including the competitors and others associated with the team, sponsors, medical staff, catering staff, media people and aircraft control and operating staff. Each morning, everyone gets back into their vehicles, airplanes, or helicopters and moves on to the next bivouac. Consequently, bivouacs are situated at airports.

Cadeau. This word means "gift" in French and has come to mean "give me a gift" in the West African countries like Burkina Faso, Mali, Senegal, and Guinea. One frequently hears this word from the local children. The most common things children ask for are pens and pencils.

Camel grass. This is a tough grass plant that thrives in the sand. When tires come onto camel grass, the motorcycle is suddenly thrust up as if it has hit a ridge. In West African desert, particularly in Mauritania, there is much camel grass. Camel grass stages are generally uncomfortable and difficult.

Camion balai. In French, *camion* means truck and *balai* means broom or sweeper truck. The camion balai truck trails along the end of the rally and collects the motorcyclists who have retired. Competitors who meet this truck are advised to retire and are taken on to the next bivouac.

Canteen. A steel box for storage of personal items. It measures one meter wide, 50 centimeters deep and 40 centimeters high. These boxes are transported by airplane for the motorcycle competitors.

Checkpoint or CP. Checkpoints are used to ensure that participants stay on the set course. The checkpoints prevent shortcuts and helps riders avoid certain border zones. Each special stage contains two or more CP's. Failure to pass through a checkpoint incurs major penalties.

Cap heading or CAP. This is a compass bearing where north is zero. The cap bearings indicate the 360 degrees around a clock face. It is one of the pieces of course information listed in the road book. Caps are listed in the road book often when there are no other clear landmarks in the desert terrain and sand dunes.

Dakar Rally. Formerly known as "The Paris Dakar Rally," the Dakar Rally is an annual professional off-road race, currently organized by the ASO. The race is open to amateur and professional entries; amateurs making about eighty percent of the participants. Despite its name, it is an off-road endurance race rather than a

conventional rally— Most of the competitive sections ("stages" or "specials") are off-road, crossing dunes, mud, camel grass, rocks, erg, among other obstacles. The distances covered vary from several kilometers to several hundred kilometers per day.

Etape. This is the French word for "stage." An étape begins at the bivouac, then to the start of special stage via the liaison, and finally on to the next bivouac via another liaison.

Fesh-fesh. This terms refers to very soft, powder-like sand. It is very easy to get stuck in fesh-fesh. Although not a sand dune, fesh-fesh are danger spots caused by many vehicles driving repeatedly over the same sandy track.

KTM. Brand name of the most popular and currently leading motorcycle in rallies today.

GPS point. The global positioning system (GPS) is a network of US-launched satellites that determine position. GPS has been used in the Dakar Rally since the system was first commercialized. Today, the use of the GPS is limited to strategic points called way points and can only offer an assistive role in route finding.

Host countries. Originally, the rally was from Paris, France to Dakar, Senegal,

interrupted by a transfer across the Mediterranean; however, due to politics and other factors, the course, including origin and destination, has been varied over the years. The rally has started from Spain, Egypt, France and Portugal.

Hubert Auriol. In 1992, Hubert Auriol won the Dakar in an automobile after having previously won the motorcycle competition on two occasions, making him the first driver to win on both two and four wheels.

Inmarsat. Satellite telephones are the lifeline of the rally administration. Records of each competitor passing a checkpoint are sent to rally headquarters and the competition results are worked out through the Inmarsat telephones. The media center is linked to the outside world through an ISDN Inmarsat network where images and documents can be transmitted. All motorcycle participants are required to carry Inmarsat mobile phones for emergency use.

Liaison. A transfer section between the special stages is called a liaison. If the participants fail to arrive within the designated time, they face a penalty. Liaison stages are often on paved roads commonly pitted with potholes and drivers cannot afford to relax. In fact, accidents are common on liaison stages.

Lunch pack. The competitors and all staff are supplied with a lunch pack every day. Its contents include a small can of pork patties, nuts, dry bread, canned mixed vegetables and some sweets.

Marathon stage. These are two-day stages driven with virtually no assistance. Because of these restrictions, the assistance vehicles cannot go to the interim bivouac. Competitors are free to perform their own maintenance within the scope of parts carried on their own vehicles.

Maximum time. This refers to the time allowed to complete a special stage. If a competitor exceeds the permitted time, penalties are added. In addition, competitors who fail to reach the start 30 minutes before their starting time are disqualified. The maximum time is set in accordance with the length and degree of difficulty of a special stage.

Optimal visual apex. This is the apex of a corner that allows the best view of oncoming traffic upon exiting the corner. It is not to be confused with the "apex of a corner" which exists at the center of the corner.

Papa Charly. "Papa Charly" is used to refer to rally headquarters when communicating by radio. Rally headquarters in Africa is a twin-engine, small jet transporter, which carries competition officials to the bivouacs each day.

Parc Fermé. *Parc* is French for "park" and refers to an area enclosed for a special purpose, while *fermé* means "closed." Vehicles are not allowed to be touched while in the parc fermé.

Penalties. Penalties are imposed by adding time, monetary fines, or in severe cases, disqualification. Penalties are imposed for various offenses, such as going over maximum time, speeding in villages and taking shortcuts that deviate substantially from the course.

Polisario Front. The rally was criticized for crossing through the disputed territory of Western Sahara between Morocco and Mauritania without consulting the Polisario Front, which is considered representative of the Sahrawi people.

Production class. This is a class in the Dakar Rally where the scope of modifications is highly restricted and the fitting of restrictors is mandatory. Speeds are not as high as in the super-production category.

Prologue. A first, short special test defining the starting order for the first stage. The time of the prologue counts for the general result.

Road Book. This is the route instruction book where the day's course is outlined on a sectional map, accompanied by cautions. The course in the Dakar Rally is completely secret. The competitors learn about the course through the information in the road book handed out the day before. Today, road books are offered in English as well as French.

Sahrawi people. These are the inhabitants of a territory of Western Sahara between Morocco and Mauritania, called the Polisario Front.

Scrutineering. Every rally starts with an inspection of persons and bikes. All team members must be accredited and all bikes must comply with the rules of the FIM.

SS. This stands for "special stage." The basis of rally competition is to pass through these stages in the shortest possible time. In Europe, the special stages are generally short, but as the race enters Africa the stages are much longer. The longest special stage in history was more than 800 kilometers.

Sand board. When a tire sinks into the sand, the crew digs it out and places the sand board under the tire to extricate the vehicle.

Super-production class. This is the top category for the four and two wheel classes. Modifications are permitted to the engine, frame and suspension. However, minimum weights in accordance with engine displacement are stipulated.

Tango. This refers to the medical teams that move around the course in four-wheel drive vehicles. Each vehicle number starts with a "T" (T1, T2 and so forth). The teams are known as "tango."

TDSPP. An acronym of "tout droit sur piste principal," which means "continue straight on the main road." These letters come up in the road book often and can sometimes mean continue straight ahead for more than 100 kilometers.

Toby Moody. The television coverage of the rally is narrated by Toby Moody, a retired motorcycle rider whose distinct English accent (especially pronouncing foreign names such as "Schless-ah", "Shi-no-zoo-ker" and "Me-oh-nee") adds to the personality of the race.

Time card. Each morning at the bivouac, competitors begin at the individual start times listed on their time cards, which are stamped at each checkpoint passed. Even when the vehicle is moved from the vehicle inspection area to the parc fermé (closed area) prior to the start for administrative reasons, the time card is used.

Truck class. Vehicles with a gross weight of 3.5 tons or more, whatever their shape, are classed as trucks. They are divided into the T4 class that participates in competition and the T5 class assistance truck that goes from bivouac to bivouac to support the competition vehicles. T4 class vehicles can undertake service activities even during special stages.

!!!. This is another abbreviation that appears in the road book. "!" means caution, indicating care is needed, and the more cautions used, the higher the level of danger. The triple caution "!!!" indicates where the highest level of caution is needed.

Quick Order Form

Email orders: www.chasingdakar.com

Postal orders: Chasing Dakar
1313 Eaton Drive
Las Vegas, NV 89102
USA

Order information:

_____ books @ $19.95 each.   **Total books:** $_____

                                                    S & H: $_____
$4.50 first book plus $2.00 each additional book.
Express shipping is available.

                                                    Total order: $_____

Credit card (*check one*):   ❐ Visa   ❐ Mastercard   ❐ AMEX   ❐ Discover

Card number number: _____

Name on card:_____

Exp. Date: _____

Ship to:

Name: _____

Address: _____

City: _____ State: _____ Zip code:_____

Telephone: _____

Email address: _____